COULD IT BE STRESS?

reflections on psychosomatic illness

Cameron Macdonald

©Argyll Publishing
First published in 1992 by
Argyll Publishing
Glendaruel
Argyll
PA22 3AE

The author has asserted his moral rights.

British Library Cataloguing-in-Publication Data.
A catalogue record for this book is available from the British
Library.

ISBN 1 874640 10 6

Cover design Marcia Clark
Typeset W W McLean, Dunoon
Linotronic output Cordfall, Civic Street, Glasgow
Printed and bound in Great Britain by Billings Book Plan Ltd,
Worcester

Feeling "stressed out" is as much a part of present-day parlance as the thrusting busy lifestyles that produce it. Yet when stress factors get to the point where people become ill, much of the medical world which relies on technological solutions seems lost for effective answers. The part played by the emotions in feeling well seems to be overlooked.

Could it be stress? based on many years of meeting sufferers of psychosomatic illness, seeks to redress the balance and tackle the part played by feelings in common health conditions.

A.Cameron Macdonald FRCP (London & Glasgow) has long experience behind him. After qualifying as a doctor in 1939 he saw service in the Royal Navy during World War ll. He served with the Royal Marines, at sea and later specialised in Aviation Medicine at the Royal Navy Air Medical School, and the RAF Institute of Aviation Medicine at Farnborough.

He became a Consultant Physician in 1958 and practiced in the Western Infirmary, Glasgow and in the Vale of Leven District General Hospital, Alexandria. A growing awareness of the connection between emotional factors and physical illness led him to take a training analysis with Dr Karl Abenheimer to qualify in psychotherapy. "The truth is," he says, "I was always more interested in the patient than the illness."

Cameron Macdonald has been for forty years Consultant Physician to the Royal Scottish Academy of Music and Drama. He was medical correspondent with The Herald for fifteen years and was Honorary President of Glasgow Psychosomatic Society.

Psychosomatic medicine is not currently in vogue... Perhaps we need it all the more but are less free to acknowledge such a need. Cameron Macdonald noticed how often physical illness was related to emotional disturbance ... He will help you make the connections.

Barbara Baird, G P and Consultant Surgeon, Essex.

(Cameron Macdonald's) book deals with psychosomatic illness in a simple way, making psychotherapy easily understandable.

The Scotsman

We started with a terribly tangled skein of wool. Untangle it, I directed, let me place myself in your hands. But he handed the ball back to me and let me unwind the wool.

former patient and sufferer from anxiety.

I was like an unfurnished room and I didn't know how to furnish it. When we talked I began to realise the things that were missing from my life... I realised how different it would have been if my mother had lived and I think I can now accept myself and the world.

former patient and asthma sufferer.

To my patients

Contents

Preface

Today then since I am in the secure possession
of leisure in a peaceable retirement, I will at length
apply myself earnestly and freely to the general
overthrow of all my former opinions.

René Descartes

Over many years my colleagues have paid me the
compliment of encouraging me to write about psychosomatic
medicine. "You must tell us what you do," they say. That is
an almost impossible task since each doctor-patient
transaction is a unique experience and depends so much on
intuitive hunches, which are as difficult to define as is the
magic of a violin concerto. Few would dispute the fact that
much of the psychodynamic literature is very heavy going
and tends to intimidate even enthusiastic enquiring minds.
When teaching undergraduates, I tried to convey the
mysteries of "sensitivity" to my students and in doing so

learned some ways of simplifying theories and approaches. I could be that an oversimplified outline may have some function and I can only plead for mercy from my more erudite psycho-analytical colleagues.

It is hoped that a greater good for future sufferers may justify this approach. To a large extent this book is a work of fiction as I have altered most of the recognisable information in the case histories so that participants may remain anonymous, while attempting to preserve the emotional essentials. Where possible, I have asked for and obtained permission to use the stories and I am surprised and grateful for the generosity of these splendid people.

I should like to acknowledge the statistical help of Dr Robin Knill-Jones and the unusual combination of secretarial and psychotherapeutic expertise of Mrs Margaret Ratcliffe. I had invaluable help in editing and criticism from Mrs Sylvia Gardner and Dr Barbara Baird. The final stages of publishing were almost painless through the efforts of Ms Cathie Thomson and Mr Derek Rodger.

Introduction

Could it be stress, doctor?" I'm asked that often. Stress is a fashionable word - almost a fashionable problem, now accepted, admissible, open to discussion. We measure workdays lost through stress-related illness; psychologists run courses in stress management. People are widely aware that illness can be stress induced; some recognise their own stress-induced factors.

But the term is wide and vague, and while some precipitant factors are stressful for everybody, others are not. One man's stress can be another's comfortable working pitch.

Within our own time, eminent researchers have identified and explored stressful behaviour patterns. Consider John

Bowlby's elegant and meticulous exploration of attachment and loss, demonstrating the clear biological impingement of emotional stress over many future years.

More recently, Friedman and Rosenman have unearthed and described "Type A" behaviour and its influence on heart disease. Later they have also begun to look at the seeds of "Type A" behaviour - the insecurity which drives high achievers.

Cameron Macdonald looks deeper and more specifically. Like much good research, his work arose through spontaneous observation. Early in his career as a Consultant in General Medicine, he noticed how often physical illness was related to emotional disturbance - often with a wide time interval; sometimes with an initial precipitant which, repeated after many years, triggered a clear and commanding illness. (The parallel with immunological illness is interesting.)

There was, at that stage, no solid body of received wisdom on the subject so, as he tells us himself, he recorded his findings and his therapy. Often this followed the lines of exposing the underlying psychological wound and, in the context of professional understanding, removing its power to impose a self-damaging life-pattern. For yesterday's coping mechanism may become to-day's self-injurious lifestyle.

Over the years Dr Macdonald has acquired invaluable (and sometimes unique) experience. Accumulating evidence has shown some clear and some evolving patterns. Now retired from NHS practice but still professionally very busy, he has gathered this experience in book form.

Psychosomatic medicine is not currently in vogue. The gentle 60s were more hospitable to these ideas than are the power-driven years of the 1980s and 90s. That, however, does not mean that we don't need it. Perhaps indeed we need it all the more but are less free to acknowledge such need.

Could it be stress?" Perhaps it could. Only connect. Cameron Macdonald, who was my boss, remains my mentor and friend. He will help you make connections.

Dr Barbara Baird MA, FRCS
General Practitioner & Consultant surgeon
Essex

1. The challenge

Twentieth Century medicine has nothing to offer this patient. Will you see him?

Consultant Physician

Over the past few decades there have been massive and rewarding improvements in the technology of medical diagnosis and treatment. There can be little doubt that great benefits have been achieved in fields such as cardiac surgery and cancer treatment. One more questionable result has been that the training of medical students has become preoccupied with this sophisticated technology and that potential undergraduates are chosen from those who show promise in the skills of mathematics, physics and chemistry. Interest in history, literature, languages and in other forms of communication tend to be disregarded and, not surprisingly, the graduate doctor finds that he has little skill in communicating with his patients or of understanding their social, cultural and emotional background.

The medical undergraduate and the practicing doctor spend endless hours elucidating the role of the cyclopenteno-phenanthrene ring, in the mysteries of hormone chemistry or in understanding the intricacies of the immune system and regard these as mandatory knowledge. Yet few are encouraged to understand the relatively simple concepts of the developmental stages through which we must all pass in childhood and adolescence, or indeed to study any of the psychological mechanisms which affect health and lifestyle.

Meanwhile a more educated and well-informed public expects and indeed demands adequate information and choice; and is ever more articulate in defining the medical profession's deficiencies. General practitioners, psychiatrists and many general physicians become aware of these gaps in their training and tend to feel confused and inadequate in their chosen profession. Some try to find a more holistic approach to their patients and may turn to alternative medicine.

It is rewarding to find that, if given a little encouragement, medical students are happy to look at the patient as well as the illness, while more and more doctors who actually look after patients are keen to acquire further skill in understanding and assessing their patient's emotional problems and correlating these with the present illness.

Two methods are commonly used in attempting to assess emotional factors in any disease. Large numbers of patients can be interrogated by means of questionnaires and the results of these are analysed to see if there are any emotional, neurotic or other factors which might have contributed to development of the disease. This method is able to demonstrate statistical information which may be valid, but the information obtained is often superficial and very frequently inconclusive.

A second method is to examine a very much smaller number of patients by a prolonged series of interviews so that some idea of the way individuals operate (their psychodynamic mechanism) is ascertained and perhaps some patterns may emerge which can be used as guides in the handling of future patients. Clearly, a busy clinician is poorly placed to organise statistically controlled material, especially in psychosomatic disease, where valid control of really important factors, such as the type of parenting, is manifestly impossible. However, it may be that the investigation of a few hundred patients in real depth will, in the long run, contribute to our knowledge of psychosomatic disease. I am aware that I immediately expose myself to the current accusation of being "merely anecdotal" and, if so, I am unashamedly anecdotal.

The family doctor is in the happy position of seeing the early stages of illness. At this point, the relevant life events may be more obvious and intervention more successful than in long-established and often habituated disease. It follows that the doctor in primary care has much to contribute in psychosomatic disorders. But who is more suited to treat the emotional aspects of psychosomatic disease at the Consultant level - the physician or the psychiatrist?

As a physician, I must admit to prejudice, but this is at least in part based on experience. My early attempts to refer psychosomatic patients to psychiatrists almost invariably resulted in an opinion that the patient was a well-balanced, hardworking and socially admirable man, who showed no evidence of anxiety or depression and whose symptoms were due to his duodenal ulcer or whatever. The fact that the patient was an obsessional perfectionist and could be making himself ill by his virtuous striving was usually overlooked. The only answer that seemed reasonable to me at the time was to have a psychotherapeutic training and to learn to treat the emotional problems as part of the general medical approach. I was privileged to have my training analysis with the late Dr Karl M Abenheimer, who was himself trained in Zurich by Carl Gustav Jung in the 1930s. Not surprisingly, psychotherapy was regarded with some suspicion by my medical and surgical colleagues, who felt that to study patients' dreams was, at best, wildly eccentric and, at worst, a complete waste of time. The psychiatrists for their part, saw this as an unwarranted intrusion into their "closed shop". Feelings of isolation at this stage were somewhat tempered by the realisation that both groups of colleagues were apparently happy to refer patients (and relatives) for opinion or treatment!

It soon became obvious that even a limited knowledge of psychodynamics was changing my approach to many aspects of my work in a hospital medical unit. The diagnosis of purely organic physical disease became more rapid and more assured, leaving time to spend on more complicated presentations. The management of all patients became more sensitive. In particular, the handling of chronic and incurable disease and of the terminally ill became easier as I felt less guilty and inadequate and, as a result, could offer better support. The diagnosis of psychosis and psychoneurosis encountered in medical wards became easier and the need to transfer such patients to the more competent care of psychiatric colleagues could be more expeditious.

My object in writing this book is to convey some of the experience garnered from an exciting clinical life, in the hope that other doctors and counsellors. may feel encouraged to help psychosomatic sufferers by using their own skills and wisdom to advance our knowledge of this relatively uncharted area.

The general public has a greater awareness of the advances and of the shortcomings of modern medicine and I hope I address general readers too, in helping to add to their understanding of their own minds and bodies.

I shall perhaps be guilty of over-simplification in my ideas of causation, classification and management, though I feel that to be a lesser evil than cloaking the psychotherapeutic process in jargon and complexity, which can only serve to discourage the beginner. One can only hope that others may be stimulated to clarify and explain many phenomena which are still clouded in obscurity, both in the science and in the psychology of these common and disabling illnesses.

2. Psychosomatic disorders

*Disease is very old and nothing about it
has changed. It is we who change as we
learn to recognise what was formerly imperceptible.*

Jean Martin Charcot

The term "psychosomatic" has had a chequered career and often seems to be in danger of meaning only what one chooses it to mean. Many clinicians use it almost as a pejorative term when they wish to imply that the patient is neurotic. However, most doctors use the term when they feel that there is a psychological component in the patient's illness.

I make so bold as to offer my own definition of a psychosomatic disorder. It is an illness in which significant emotional factors combine with physical and genetic factors to produce an illness which can be demonstrated by clinical, radiological, laboratory or other techniques to have produced structural changes in the body. This definition excludes patients who are mentally ill in the sense of psychoneurosis, as these do not show "organic" physical changes.

Some very experienced physicians have suggested that psychosomatic patients are producing an illness which is partly a defence against a true psychiatric illness such as depression. I would agree that some conditions such as a heart attack are almost a sophisticated kind of suicide and certainly many patients with psychosomatic disease must work through a spell of depression before becoming well. I tend nevertheless to make a distinction between psychoneurosis and psychosomatic illness. It is often helpful in this context to look for secondary gain, where the patient appears to achieve some advantage from the illness. This phenomenon is very rare, though not unknown in psychosomatic medicine, while it is extremely common in psychoneurosis and particularly among hysterics.

It might seem as if our life is a journey along a road which is at times sunny and relaxing and at other times stormy and threatening. If the journey becomes too difficult, we reach a point at which the road divides and we have a choice of two ways at this "Y" junction. Some may choose the road to neurosis developing symptoms which, albeit without their conscious knowledge, allow them to avoid the situations which are too difficult to face. Others, for reasons of personality and previous experience, choose the other road and strive even harder to overcome the obstacles. They may do this by working longer hours, or by even being more meticulous about punctuality and attention to detail. Sooner or later this effort produces a physical (psychosomatic) illness, which is often potentially lethal. The only "secondary gain" for psychosomatic patients is discomfort, pain or death. They appear to make themselves ill by trying too hard. Fortunately, the capacity to confront their own behaviour is often surprising. The consequent rewards of a psychotherapeutic approach are often speedy and satisfying for both patient and doctor.

To understand the psychosomatic disorders, it may be helpful to classify them into groups and three such groups seem relevant and practical.

The first group of disorders produces symptoms or illnesses which are **symbolic** of their stresses and are often expressed in body language. Patients may have experienced rejection in early life - such as is experienced by adopted or fostered children and in single parent families; or if one parent works away from home as in sea-going occupations. Spells in hospital or early separation to boarding school, especially if the parents are abroad, are interpreted as rejection, though it is almost never articulated and may never reach conscious awareness. Such patients react to later rejection by symptoms at times paradoxically symbolic of the process by recurrent vomiting, diarrhoea, or repeated spontaneous abortions. In Great Britain there is pressure upon children, especially males, that they should not show grief by weeping and it is interesting, if not surprising, that these individuals are prone to water retention syndromes such as angio-oedema or periodic water retention. Common figurative expressions serve to illustrate the inherent symbolism as "he makes me sick", "she's a pain in the neck" or "I'm scared stiff".

The other two groups seem to respond to stress in a fashion that may depend on their own concept of their body image. There appear to be people who see their own identity as the reflection they see in the mirror and acquire a kind of externalised body image. When they are under stress, their symptoms and illnesses are also externalised and the result is a **disturbance of their external appearance** or structure; as in obesity, anorexia nervosa, musculo-skeletal and joint disorders and skin disease.

The third group of patients are those that **internalise their body image.** When pressured, they internalise this stress and respond with internal symptoms. If threatened or angry, they maintain a calm front by bottling up their feelings, but they "clench their fists" inside themselves. This internal fist clenching often results in spasm of circular smooth muscle in blood vessels or viscera. This is seen in many conditions characterised by circular muscle contraction as in migraine, coronary heart disease, hypertension, asthma, pylorospasm or spastic colon. An important part of the therapeutic process is to help such people to express their anger and resentment rather than to "bottle-up".

These classifications must only act as broad guide-lines to aid our understanding, since there is, in reality, often a considerable overlap within the categories. An asthmatic may, for example, also suffer from eczema, so it is "internalising" and "externalising" simultaneously. Indeed my own interests in the psychosomatic aspects of rheumatoid arthritis was aroused when patients suffering from this disease were referred to me with peptic ulcers, which had apparently resulted from their medication. They, too, show that these classifications are not necessarily mutually exclusive.

It has been suggested that links can be drawn between certain personalities, or particular social and emotional events and the psychosomatic disorders these will produce. While my experience tells me that this is broadly the case, I am all too aware of the dangers of generalisation in an area where no two cases can ever be the same. Some idea of the likely constellation of events in each illness is a help in the management of the patient in that time may be saved in knowing what to expect and where to explore in their life history. But emphatically these expectations must only be used as guidelines and used with circumspection and sensitivity or the pitfalls of observer error will be compounded by preconceived ideas.

Each person is a unique individual with unique problems and cannot be treated by generalisations - albeit thereby only becoming an anecdote!

Many would claim that events like early parental loss affect people who do not develop psychosomatic disorders or other illnesses. This is certainly true, but the relevance of this type of early trauma depends on how it was handled and discussed at the appropriate time and it takes experience and sensitivity to assess its importance or unimportance in later illnesses. The doctor or therapist must acquire the skill and sensitivity to share the feelings of the patient about the experiences and so to assess their significance. Perhaps at best this type of assessment is rather like a weather forecast and we have often to wait to confirm the direction from which the storm arrived.

Personality characteristics and previous life events do appear to offer some guidance in the common psychosomatic disorders and these will be discussed under the appropriate headings in later chapters. Social, religious and cultural differences may modify attitudes in different areas and countries, so that the clinician has the exciting challenge of discovering the correct weighting of life events for the patients in his own locality.

If we are to understand psychosomatic illness, it may be helpful to recognise some of the ways in which people may react to emotional stress.

1. Identification Since all young children do most of their learning by imitation, it is likely that their personality, behaviour and illnesses will reflect the people they imitated and with whom they identify.

The first people we encounter are our parents, so we tend to use them as a yardstick by which we measure all the others we meet in life. If we are lucky, we stop to consider whether the yardstick gave long or short measure and can accept with equanimity and indeed amusement both the "good" and the "bad" in our own parents. The insecure individuals try only to be the "good" parent and repress and hide the "bad" parent. In later life they meet situations in which they identify themselves with the "bad" parent as, for example, when they have to dismiss an employee and they feel inappropriately guilty. This feeling of guilt may well render them vulnerable to illness.

Identification with one's parents may be a scientific reality as in disorders with a true genetic component like duodenal ulcer. Or it may be merely contagious as in asthma, where a parent often had chronic respiratory disease though not necessarily asthma itself. (That this is not truly genetic is seen in the case of adopted children developing allergies or asthma by identification with their adopted parent). Patients also identify with parental personality patterns such as obsessional traits of rigidity, punctuality or religiosity. They also identify unconsciously with time scales like anniversaries and with locations which have unpleasant associations. I had one family where both father and son developed a heart attack in the same railway station.

2. Reactivation of childhood experience is common. The panic a defenceless child feels in bereavement or even of being lost in a supermarket seems to imprint a tape, which can be re-run in vaguely similar situations in adult life. Clearly as adults these people could cope adequately, but the feeling of helpless panic is that of the helpless child and is as devastating as it is apparently inexplicable. So as the doctor or counsellor listens, he must practice geometry, looking for parallels and angles, since once aware of the earlier event, the patient can learn to switch off the inappropriate tapes. Any childhood emotional stress, often totally forgotten, can trigger off this reaction - early hospitalisation, adoption, sexual assault, divided loyalty, sibling rivalry or apparent banishment to boarding school are common starting points for later difficulties.

3. Rejection is a feeling inculcated so early in life that it is a recurring mechanism that deserves special, if recurring, mention. The baby in his pram knows he can attract his mother's attention by smiles and gurgles; but if the telephone rings and the mother turns away, the child, not knowing about telephones, feels he has induced his mother's rejection. This rejection is an unpleasant feeling in itself, but many people also fear that they are responsible for inducing it. In order to protect themselves, they may choose to do the rejecting first. This is a familiar mechanism in terms of even normal behaviour. A teenager will put his parents to the test by trying to see how much obstreperous behaviour they will tolerate before they reject him. A similar process occurs in psychosomatic ailments. The young woman who fears that no one will like her, develops facial acne so that the lads will be "put off" from the very start. In this way the possibility of a later, still more painful rejection, is forestalled.

4. Body language is a recurring mechanism which expresses the underlying emotional stress and is a useful diagnostic tool. The psychosomatic disorders classified under symbolic diseases should exemplify this mechanism. Heart ache is a fairly classic example, but dysphagia may merely indicate an emotional situation which the patient feels he cannot swallow. The secretary who fears dismissal if she objects to her employer's unreasonable behaviour has constantly to "bite her tongue" and reports to her doctor with a painful tongue.

5. Displacement as I see it, is when a patient tries to acquire an illness to displace it from a loved and dependent figure, especially if he feels his behaviour has contributed to the illness. An eighteen year old girl appeared at my outpatient clinic with a three weeks history of chest pain, suggestive of ischaemic heart disease, a highly unlikely diagnosis. I said to her, "Haven't I seen you before?" and she replied, "Yes, you came to our house a month ago when my mother had a heart attack."

6. Retaliation There is often an element of self-punishment in this kind of displacement, especially as all young children believe that their parents will remain well as long as they are good, polite and obedient. If they feel angry with a parent, they invariably believe that the parent will become ill or even die. Obviously this negative feeling is repressed and it may erupt years later if either parent takes ill or dies. The resultant psychosomatic disorder may well be a self-punishment ritual.

If there is a strong element of guilt, the Talion Law of "an eye for an eye and a tooth for a tooth" comes into play and the "retaliation" is that the patient may suffer a fate similar to that of the patient. An Ear, Nose and Throat surgeon referred a clergyman, who had already consulted six surgeons in a space of a few months, because he was suffering from swallowing difficulties. It transpired that, when the patient was eighteen years old, his father had developed a carcinoma of his gullet. When he visited his father in hospital, the ward sister had insisted that the father was not trying to swallow and asked my patient to make him drink a cup of soup. He tried to do so and his father died during the attempt. Not surprisingly the son felt he should be punished by suffering a similar fate.

7. Reality versus fantasy Normal people may have experienced times of quite incredible hardship or misfortune and yet appear to be relatively undamaged by the experience. It may be that, apart from being secure and constitutionally strong individuals, the reason for their survival is that the suffering was real and related to a finite situation. There are spells when we experience real fear due to a real situation of danger but the feeling of fear goes when the danger passes.

In contrast, we become anxious in situations where we anticipate disaster without there being any real reason for it. It is this potential crisis which induces anxiety or even physical illness. Many patients develop symptoms related to fantasy stress and must be helped to differentiate real from potential hazards. For example, the mother who fears death and disaster if her child is late home from school suffers great anxiety and yet would deal with a real crisis with calm competence.

I remember one man who had an irritable colon syndrome with a severe exacerbation of symptoms in the middle of each month. He ran his own business and had developed a habit of predicting the financial implication of his month's trading around the middle of the month. This was the time of his physical relapse. At the end of the month, he was symptom-free, regardless of whether he made a loss or a profit!

8. Obsessionalism The "virtuous obsessional" was the description given by Dr J L Halliday (13) of his psychosomatic patients. This is often described nowadays as "Type A" personality (Friedman and Roseman (14)). These people often had a strict and rigid upbringing, where cleanliness and punctuality were of paramount importance. School reports were scrutinised with assiduity and concern and late hours in the teenage years were discouraged. Early life was characterised by a singular lack of physical contact or demonstrative affection. They can seldom recall having sat on a parent's knee. Early parental death occurred commonly in such patients.

This upbringing leaves them in doubt as to their capacity to be loved or to love and they tend to compensate for this emotional dubiety by denying their dependency needs and acquiring a veneer of pseudo-independence. They feel they must be intellectually and professionally successful, so work hard to achieve positions of responsibility and authority, preferably where they will be unlikely to experience criticism. In the upper social strata they aim to become the company chairman or to occupy a professorial chair or the pulpit. Further down this social scale they become overhead crane drivers or lighthouse keepers - isolated yet controlling.

9. Unresolved mourning I am greatly indebted to Dr J W Paulley (15) who introduced me to the importance of this concept as a common mechanism in psychosomatic disorders. Adult patients, who in childhood experience bereavement, often the death of a parent or sibling, may never have had an opportunity to to work through their mourning process. A subsequent bereavement or its equivalent reactivates the earlier unresolved mourning with the possibility of a major emotional crisis or the development of any of the diseases associated with immuno-suppression, since it is known that bereavement in itself lowers our immune defences (Bartropp et al (16)). Autoimmune disorders can then gain a foothold so this is always a possible background to disorders like haemolytic anaemia, collagen disorders and ulcerative colitis.

We should remember that in this context "bereavement" is in inverted commas and may not imply an actual death. Vulnerable people with a previous unresolved mourning will react to a broken engagement, a spontaneous abortion, a stillbirth, retiral or redundancy and even to the loss of a much valued household pet.

3. Psychodynamic models

I would know my shadow and my light,
so shall I at last be whole.
Then courage, brother, dare the grave passage.
Here is no final grieving, but an abiding hope.

Michael Tippett.

Reading books on psychological theory can be useful but purely intellectual and theoretical knowledge is less helpful than being able to apply book learning to the problems and clients with whom we are already working. Much credit must go to Freud (4) as the pioneer in this field, with his well-known concepts of the "id", the "ego" and the "super-ego". I like to imagine Freud's idea of a human psyche as a house with the conscious identity, the ego occupying the living quarters, the unconscious id lurking in the basement and the super-ego, a kind of conscience installed in the attic. Freud suggested that much personal conflict arose from the struggle between primitive desires and acceptable social behaviour. I wonder if he did not have too negative a view of the id. It surely must be the source of many new and creative ideas. Certainly in psychosomatic disorders we often see the super-ego as too powerful, acting as a crushing Atlas-like structure so that anything worth doing becomes immoral, illegal or fattening! In the psychosomatic field, Freud's most useful contribution may be his views on orality and the importance of the mouth and of feeding, especially in relation to dependency problems. His ideas of anal aggression and its association with both power and anger are also vitally important in understanding a great deal of gastrointestinal disease.

The devotees of Transactional Analysis (3) have successfully used and modified a Freudian model to express different kinds of human interaction. They suggest that people relate to one another at one of three levels: as one adult to another; as an adult to a child; or as an adult to a superior authority figure. This is a readily understandable and practical concept.

The Jungian model (4) suggests a balance between opposing forces. In Jung's view, we must be prepared to accept both the positive and the negative aspects of our personalities. Otherwise, as in an electrical circuit, there will be no light, warmth or power. To enjoy the sunshine we must accept the inevitability of shadows.

A multi-dimensional model can be a useful simplification of these ideas. On the vertical axis we have the intellect of all the thinking functions balanced at the lower end by the emotional and feeling functions. We all know logical people who must have an intellectual explanation for everything and who are often insensitive to other people's feelings and viewpoints. They are rather like old-fashioned newspaper cartoons, all head and no body, and are therefore top heavy and easily upset by criticism. In contrast is the wobble-about toy of the nursery with inbuilt stability as exemplified by the happy, relaxed and secure working man with a real interest in his children.

On the horizontal axis we have purely sensory function at the right end - the ability to manipulate a hammer and screwdriver and to understand shape and texture, balanced on the far left by a sense of intuition and perception of how people feel.

Ideally we should have a mixture of all four functions and Jung advised us to locate the strong functions and then to try to improve the opposite ones, which are often deficient in their contribution. Men tend to be intellectual and dextrous and have to be encouraged to use their feeling and intuition. Women are often much better at feelings and sensitivity and usually reach the right conclusion for what appears, to the logical male , to be the wrong reasons.

To complete our model, in the third dimension is extraversion/introversion. The extravert is the salesman who can talk to anyone and can convince them with his patter - much froth and little beer. The introverted are less communicative and more withdrawn but are splendid value once we get to know them, as they possess great depths of artistry and creativity. Perhaps the middle ground is again the ideal. When we look at ourselves and other people, we find that to some extent we are all a multi-faceted self with many qualities and attributes and real maturity consists in giving place to all the functions and integrating them into a whole and therefore a healthy person.

We have also to come to terms with our true sexuality. Since we are all the product of two parents we must accept some of the qualities of both. In western society rigid notions as to male and female roles have become more relaxed in recent years. It is now no longer regarded as the female "prerogative" to clean the house or change the nappies, nor does the idea of a female engineer or bus driver raise many eyebrows. As a result, young men are becoming more able to express the inherently "feminine" aspects of their personalities, their sensitivity and emotions. Women too, happily wear trousers without feeling or looking less feminine and can learn to change a wheel or fly an aircraft without jeopardising their female image. However, we still encounter in our work men and women of all ages who are so insecure in their sexual identity that they feel the need to suppress in themselves those qualities which they have inherited from the parent of the opposite sex. It is my impression that this dilemma is commoner in males, who consequently have to over-compensate by being supermen to project a "macho" image. The well-integrated man has no need to put on such an act and is inherently more stable and resilient. The female part of a man often appears in his poetry, painting or dreams as a familiar girl, whom Jung called the "anima" since it is what "animates" him. The "anima" often figures in a young man's dreams as a coloured girl (the female shadow) sitting on his left, giving him wise advice.

Girls have a corresponding male "animus", often multiple, in their dreams. The woman who doubts or resents her feminine role is said to be animus-possessed and at some level wishes she were a male. She has to diminish or destroy all the men she encounters, as in the term "animosity". Freud called this the penis-envy syndrome but perhaps failed to notice that men can equally envy women their capacity to bear children and their general sensitivity and wisdom.

Many people find it important to value only the positive aspects of their personality and behaviour and it is common to attempt to deny the negative and sinister qualities. This persistent denial can result in acts of discourtesy or insensitivity without their even being noticed. If we are to become "whole", we have to give our devils house-room. Then, as allies rather than enemies, they have warmth and power to put at our disposal. Deny the shadow and we are in danger of being demon-possessed. Accept it, and we can get up to devilment and enjoy our mischief.

These early Freudian and Jungian models have been both

supported and decried by many subsequent workers and writers, but all have added further useful ideas which can increase our understanding of the complexity of human behaviour. Some suggestions for further reading are noted in the bibliography.

As time has passed psychotherapists and counsellors have tended to become more adaptable and eclectic and to use ideas from all the schools of psychological thought. It is perhaps important to remember that in counselling what we are is much more important than what we say!

For the beginner who wishes to use a psychotherapeutic approach to his patients there is something to be said for choosing just a few patients and spending some time with them. It is wise at this stage to have a colleague with whom to discuss the transactions and interactions but, in the end, it is mainly from our patients that we learn. I can hear the family doctor protest that there is no time to spend on such luxury. It was the late Dr Michael Balint (3) who pointed out that the doctor can spend five to ten minutes every week, or every fortnight, on one patient over his whole working life. Alternatively, he can set aside one hour to see this patient and thereby has a good chance of solving the problem permanently. Apart from the benefit to the patient, a great deal of working time can be saved.

4. Developmental Stages I

You may give them your love but not your thoughts,
For they have their own thoughts.
You may house their bodies but not their souls,
For their souls dwell in the house of tomorrow,
Which you cannot visit, not even in your dreams.
You may strive to be like them, but seek not to make them like
you.

Kahil Gibran

Just as physical development progresses in an ordered
sequence, so too growing up emotionally has recognised
stages, through which we must all pass. An understanding of
these stages, and how we may falter in our progress through
them is essential, if we are to grasp some of the problems
which arise in adult life.

I like to consider these stages broadly under three headings,
as the developing child recognises first "me", then "I" and
finally "everyone".

When we are stressed, pressurised or ill, we may regress to an
earlier stage of emotional development. If we can recognise

that this is what is happening to our patients, friends, ourselves... the resulting puzzling behaviour may be more readily understood.

Before considering these stages of life, it is pertinent to discuss the influences affecting the baby before birth. We are only slowly acquiring evidence of the influences at work in intra-uterine life since they are so difficult to evaluate and substantiate. It has been postulated that foetal life may well be a time of stress which should be considered in some patients.

It is tempting to believe that the most comfortable time in our life was in the womb, enjoying warmth and the comfort of hydraulic suspension in the amniotic fluid, while being constantly fed, protected and orchestrated. The subsequent emergence into a cold brilliantly lit and uncomfortable world may seem highly unpleasant to the baby. It is perhaps not surprising that we find a warm bath so relaxing and are renewed and invigorated by the hours spent in the comfort of bed, a culturally acceptable form of near pre-birth luxury.

It has been suggested that mothers who are happy, secure and excited about the rewards and challenges of childbearing have children who are relaxed and easy, in their infancy at least. Mothers who are unwilling childbearers or who are stressed by environmental pressures, (particularly if a termination has been attempted and failed), may produce a child who seems anxious and unhappy from birth. It has even been suggested that children whose fathers have died or deserted the mother during pregnancy, have a sense, conscious or unconscious, of rejection, which may affect their subsequent behaviour. It is difficult to know whether any messages reach them before birth, or whether they are influenced by their mother's later comments or attitudes.

If the mother dies in childbirth, the surviving child is often aware of feeling that he or she is to blame for the mother's death, with results ranging from self-punishment rituals to an understandable fear of pregnancy or of inducing pregnancy. It has been noted that a very long and difficult labour is fairly common in the early history of claustrophobics and, for them, birth may be a welcome release from "confinement". So there may be times when we must try to take our patients back to their earliest possible memories as the late Dr Frank Lake (12) has advised in his writings.

"Me" From birth until somewhere around three to five years of age the child does not see himself (or herself) as an individual but rather as an extension of the mother. He will say, "This is John's teddy bear". During this stage the child feels it is essential that he has the whole attention of the mother or surrogate mother. He imagines his mother's love as a searchlight which leaves him totally lost and in the dark if it is not directed towards him. If mother has to give attention to her husband or to the other members of the family the child "acts out", a term often used to describe the behaviour of hysterics. He directs his anger outward by crying, shouting, kicking or throwing things.

If he feels reasonably secure, he learns to tolerate interruptions in his mother's total caring. He separates himself from her and begins to accept his individual identity. At this stage the normally developing, secure child may cause parental anxiety by running off on his own when out for a walk, in contradistinction to the insecure child, who continually clings to the parent.

It appears the most vital ingredient in achieving a secure child is that he is handled and cuddled frequently by his parents. This allows him to see the world as a friendly place and himself as worthy and capable of contact and communication. If he has little personal contact with his parents, he reasons that he is not cuddled because he is unlovable. He cannot understand that his parents are just undemonstrative by nature or are too busy attending to other matters. He assumes he is unworthy of their attention. He may grow up convinced he is an emotional failure and later may compensate for his inadequacies by intellectual and industrial success and by isolated pseudo-independence - "I don't need people." A child who has had to have a spell in hospital in early childhood may, in later life, equate illness with punishment and regard doctors and hospitals as hostile "institutions". These children are often the adults who develop cancer phobia when they feel guilty, or whose blood pressure rises at the sight of a stethoscope.

In cases of early deprivation personality disorders may arise. The individual may fail to progress to the next developmental stage and continue to behave like a three-year-old, acting out his or her anger by stealing, stabbing or bombing. Like three-year-olds these people have not developed a moral sense to distinguish right from wrong. However, it is important to be able to differentiate those who never progress beyond this infantile behaviour pattern from those who only temporarily regress to this early stage, as in the "acting out" of hysterical people. Temporary regression may be therapeutic in so far as it offers an opportunity to evaluate the life situation at that early age. Missing or forgotten pieces of childhood can be identified and can be used to modify adult feelings and so improve both tolerance and general wellbeing.

The very young child fears separation from the parents, but in the external world is also afraid of things he cannot handle and manipulate so is afraid of fire, water, darkness, and wind. Most children find that they can play in and use water and become reassured, but it is interesting these childish fears often persist into adult life in many people.

"I" From somewhere between three and five years the average child begins to develop an individual identity and has gradually to work out his (or her) personal qualities, strengths and weaknesses. The fifteen or sixteen year old should have a clear and acceptable picture of himself to carry into the joys, challenges and responsibilities of the adult world.

In the first stages of what I have called the "I" process, the child begins to develop a conscience and to understand that his immediate needs may have to "wait their turn" in the family setting. Rather than "acting out", as did the toddler, he now turns his frustration inward, often becoming uncommunicative, anxious and depressed, but he realises that his mother is a lighthouse rather than a fixed searchlight beam, and that he will get attention in due course. However, he still feels small and vulnerable and so must regard his parents, who seem large and strong by contrast, as always good, right and just, regardless of their actual behaviour. If the parent falls short of perfection by turning off the television or dispatching the offspring to bed, the child represses the "bad" parent. This repression, in the young child, of his own hostile feelings towards his parents seems to stem from the belief that, if he hates or resents them, they will become ill or die. Magic rituals are often employed to ward off this evil fate, such as touching or clinging. These rituals occasionally reappear in very ill adult patients, who have to touch the doctor to keep him safe in their hour of need.

It helps to reassure the child that a little hate is merely the other side of the coin of love and is perfectly acceptable. Later the youngsters come to realise that the opposite of love is not hatred but indifference. The parental role at this stage is to define boundaries for the child. These may be physical, as in not stepping off the pavement, or emotional, as in not punching little sister! There should, however, be adequate freedom within the boundaries. If no limits are set, the child is never sure of what is acceptable and becomes understandably confused. If the routine is too strict in terms of cleanliness, punctuality and performance generally, there is danger of producing an obsessional, to whom, in later life, minor and inevitable mistakes become disasters.

It is important to remember that for at least seven or eight years most children take all statements at their face value and do not understand the intricacies of metaphor. If a mother says, "You'll be the death of me", this is taken literally and reinforces the barely conscious fear in the child that his misbehaviour is capable of provoking his mother's illness or death. So as parents we must be vigilant and choose our words carefully. I recall one middle-aged lady whose life had been ruined by feelings of inadequacy and poor self-evaluation. She could still remember how, when she was a toddler, she had accompanied her mother who was pushing a pram containing her newly born sister. As neighbours stopped to admire the new arrival, the mother repeatedly said, "Just another mouth to feed".

Of course children gradually learn to distinguish the literal from the metaphorical and to enjoy the phantasies of Father Christmas and fairy tales. They need to use these ideas to widen their own creative and imaginative potential.

During the first decade the progress of emotional growth may be affected by the addition of further children to the family. Except in the case of twins or other multiple pregnancy, the eldest child is also an only child for part of his life. The appearance of a second child inevitably comes as something of a shock to the child who has hitherto had his parents all to himself. He may become incontinent, like the new baby, so that he can receive similar attention. It is important that parents recognise how difficult this time is for their older child and should allow him to express his resentment. It is interesting how it is the immediately younger sibling who is often the most disliked in the ranks of even large families. The only child has the advantage of not doubting the parental love and interest and has not the discomfort of having to share his parents with brothers or sisters. Nevertheless the long-term disadvantages of remaining an only child may be considerable. Only children are late in learning to share and may suffer spells of loneliness and isolation. A surprising number are told, or may imagine, that the single child family was a direct result of their being unrewarding or that they had threatened the mother's life during pregnancy or delivery. Some suffer as a result of being bombarded by all the parents' expectations which are not spread over a larger family. In adult life they have often to carry the load of elderly or sick parents without the support of a brother or sister.

It should also be noted that many young children think parents can choose the sex of their offspring. In a family of one son and two younger daughters, the son may feel that he was a disappointment to his parents and that they chose the other sex for the subsequent children. This undeserved feeling of inadequacy may persist into adult life.

In families with three children the middle child is often obsessionally well behaved. In early life the child in this position feels the oldest gets special privileges in clothes and toys while the youngest is favoured as the baby. So to be noticed he has to be clean, punctual and generally agreeable.

The youngest child is often subjected to unconscious pressures to remain a child, especially as an emotional lifeline for vaguely unsatisfactory parental relationships. He may have to fight quite strongly to cut this umbilical cord to escape into his own adult destiny.

With luck, by the age of ten or thereabouts, the child is secure enough to accept that his mother does not always need to be "good", and so the " bad" mother has no longer to be swept under the carpet. Some criticism of the mother's cooking, hairstyle or clothes emerges and is usually accepted with equanimity and indeed with relief. The youngster then says to himself, "Mother, whom I love and respect, is not perfect, so my friends will not mind if I am sometimes less than perfect." What a relaxing experience! So the youngster can step out and do more adventurous things.

By this time the uncommunicative stage of latency is passing and the ten to twelve year olds often demonstrate quite remarkable insight, honesty and understanding, though, before long, cultural and social conventions again tend to inhibit frankness.

In the early teens there is usually the phase of "homosexuality" in that the youngster exclusively seeks the company of others of the same sex and at the same time "rejects" the opposite sex. This is also frequently a narcissistic stage in which the young person is preoccupied with external appearances, perhaps aware of the need to "cover up" the inner chaos. If this type of behaviour persists into adult life, the outward air of perfection is decorative and often attractive to the opposite sex, but if the "immaculate" state has to be maintained constantly, relaxation and warmth tend to be inhibited. When the mother has been accepted as being fallible, the father is subjected to more careful scrutiny. His strengths and weaknesses are assessed realistically and this makes it easier for the youngster to understand the variabilities of the adults with whom he will work and play in the future.

In his turn a father must be brought down to size by being found out to be fallible, otherwise adult status cannot be reached. It is regrettable that men may take criticism less easily than women and if the father is insecure and has to stand on his dignity we see the makings of teenage rebellion. Most youngsters start politely and indeed humourously. I recall chiding my youngest for asking for a drink of orange without saying "please" and in reply to my "What do you say?" big brother chipped in with "Say "waiter"."

If the father protests, the teenager's behaviour becomes even more outrageous. How well this group knows the most fruitful way of exploiting a father's Achilles' heel! They become involved in disapproved religions or join the most inappropriate political party or whatever will cause the maximum uproar. If the father is sensible, he will admit to his frailties. Peace will soon reign and the youngster may say not too unkindly, "You're past it, Dad; I'll mow the lawn." In his famous TV interview with John Freeman, Carl Gustav Jung was asked at what age he became an adult and he replied, "I found my father fallible when I was twelve."

"Everyone" Having found both parents fallible, the young people can probably accept that they too have defects, but that these are acceptable and do not necessarily exclude them from success in life. They have completed their blueprint of themselves and are satisfied with the resulting picture. It is interesting that the Biblical exhortation to "love thy neighbour as thyself" underlies the necessity to like ourselves.

Again, there are events which can cause adults to regress for short periods to the "I" stage resulting in behaviour which varies from being merely self-centred and demanding to quite severe anxiety and depression. There are, of course, people who never really leave this stage and spend their lives in a permanent state of self doubt, self depreciation and insecurity, with poor tolerance of the demands and challenges of normal life.

The major hazard of the transition from infancy to adulthood is the loss of one or other parent. The girl whose mother dies may have difficulty in completing her feminine identity or if she is the eldest of the family, may feel thrust (too early) into adult responsibilities and try to be both wife and daughter to her widowed father. Much depends on the child's age and whether, by the time of the bereavement, her mother had been seen as fallible. The youngster must have a chance to talk about the loss and to mourn and be reassured that her mother's death was not her fault, as she invariably believes. Too often the death is not discussed - back to school and get on with it - and a time-bomb of unresolved mourning is left ticking with potentially dangerous results.

If her father dies, the girl feels less confident in the male world and may feel a need to remain in a female environment. She may say, "I nearly became a nun." It is probable that she still considered her father as "perfect" and so she will have an unrealistic expectation of men. Such young women often marry a much older man as a substitute father rather than as a husband. Immense potential problems can result from such a marriage since the husband must, of course, be perfect and as a substitute father may constitute something of an incestuous threat.

The young male is, of course, equally upset by his mother's death and if she died before her fallibility was accepted, the lad grows up expecting female perfection. He may not be able to tolerate female demands and female sexuality and may become homosexual, to avoid the threat. Again, he may eventually marry a much older woman. If the father dies, the son may take on his role and find means of supporting the family by taking on paper rounds and other part-time posts. These young men tend to identify with the "good" father and try hard to fulfil that role. They have often two jobs in adult life, so as to be good providers. They have rarely had an opportunity to learn to use leisure time for relaxation and play.

5. Developmental stages II

The best thing the parent can give to his offspring is the priceless boon of non-interference.

Helton G Baynes

We might say that the point at which a young person can regard both his parents as fallible is the moment at which he has completed the task of forming his own identity. This is a useful guideline in clinical assessment, or indeed, when interviewing potential employees. I remember asking a young lady at an interview if she saw her father as fallible and she immediately replied, "Fallible, of course he's fallible; I wish you could meet him, he's great." But while a vital milestone has been reached we must hope that the process of growth continues throughout our whole life so that we may go forward searching and exploring for new ideas and insights.

During the development of the identity we are subjected to many pressures from parents, teachers, religious advisers and so on. We may accept these models and restrictions and conform to an identity which is acceptable socially though it is in some ways a false identity or mask. Jung calls this the persona and points out that in early adulthood we have often to tackle the task of dismantling the false self to become our true self.

The path of continuing growth is strewn with challenges and hazards. Perhaps the most important decision of life is the choice of marriage partner. One common, if totally unconscious, pitfall is that unless he has a very secure and realistic assessment of his parents, the young man will marry someone who reminds him of his mother and the young lady someone resembling her father. Problems may arise as they project on to the puzzled spouse qualities and often defects which he or she does not possess but which belong to the parent. The potential sexual complications are obvious.

Another problem is that young men tend to idealise their fianceés to the point of fantasy and imbue them with desired, but impossible, qualities. Some inevitable, but inescapable, disappointments will arise in the future. In some parts of Africa the marriage ceremony is much more realistic than the conventional Western vows. The young couple are asked in turn, "Do you know this man's good points and his bad points and are you prepared to live with both together in the same house?"

Perhaps the most useful requirements for the successful marriage are that each partner should be "adult" and able to communicate both verbally and non-verbally. Preferably they should laugh at the same things and thus be able to share the probable disasters.

Having children is a surprising threat to some parents though it is the ultimate joy and reward for most. Insecure men are upset that they have to share their wife with the new arrival. As one surprisingly enlightened man said after the birth of a son, "I felt she was away with another man." There seems little doubt that having children gives us a new attitude and respect for our own parents and if growth is proceeding we can learn to care not only for our own family but for an extended family of dependants, employees, neighbours, clients and patients.

Middle age produces its own problems. Both men and women often reach a point at which their life-long ambitious striving reaches its zenith and they feel they have no likelihood of further progress. The path over the next ten to twenty years to retiral seems to loom ahead as boring and frustrating. Some will decide that they must somehow make money as a new goal of power - others will become involved in committees to wield another form of power. The more secure and enlightened accept the situation and decide to improve their golf, buy a boat or learn a new hobby and are glad to relinquish some of the striving. The latter group, not surprisingly, tend to outlive the others!

For many years the menopause has been used by doctors as a convenient diagnostic escape route when faced with almost any obscure symptomatology in women aged thirty to sixty. So persistently has this device been used that the label has become accepted even by the patients. In fact it seems likely that most women who have had a normal and fulfilling reproductive life cope without symptoms. It is perhaps understandable that childless women see the climacteric as the disappearance of their last chance and are angry and in some cases also guilty, indeed flushed with resentment. Some feel that this milestone will cause their "men to pause" and fear, totally unnecessarily, they will be less attractive.

The time of the menopause often coincides with the point at which the fledglings are leaving the next. This loss of those who represent such a major physical and emotional investment is underlined by the loss of the ability to have more children. As a result this point may be seen as an "end" rather than a "transition". Some re-adjustment and re-orientation is necessary, especially if the marital relationship has lost some if its magic, and communication has faltered during the exhausting years of parenthood. The menopause both symbolises and accentuates the mid-life crisis, rather than causing it. Nowadays many women will still be in mid-career at the time of the menopause, and may be too busy to notice its minor physical inconveniences. If they do have time on their hands, once their children have left home, they often discover a latent creativity which, no longer needed for procreation, can be developed in other directions.

The loss of one's employment or retiral are to some extent a "bereavement" and how the individual responds depends on his or her previous experience of bereavement and its resolution. For the housewife the husband's retiral may be quite threatening as she does not retire and may still have to produce three meals a day. It is a good idea to celebrate one's fiftieth birthday by sitting down and planning retiral. Decision making is less easy at sixty or sixty-five and we need time to organise a fulfilling life for all the household when this major change in lifestyle occurs. There is some statistical evidence that a man who retires or who is made redundant without having a rewarding hobby, a part-time job or other raison d'être has a relatively short life span regardless of his age at retiral (or redundancy). Fortunate indeed are those who can go on learning, accepting new ideas and enjoying new challenges throughout their whole lives.

6. Psychotherapy

*Nature has given man one tongue, but two ears
that we may hear twice as much as we speak.*

Epictetus

*As a grown man you should know better than go
around advising people.*

Bertholt Brecht

For the uninitiated the process known as psychotherapy is difficult to understand or even to imagine, despite the fact that many ordinary people have experienced the benefits of talking to a good listener, be it the barman, the hairdresser or a friend.

Trained counsellors in the caring professions have tried to improve the acuity and span of their listening to assess the feelings as well as the facts in the narrator's history. The qualities required appear to be, essentially, an intuitive gift combined with a capacity for genuine caring, sincerity and confidentiality. Training is invaluable since there are rules and techniques which help to avoid the many emotional pitfalls in such a deep and close relationship. Ideally the counsellor should be sufficiently aware of his or her own emotional problems and "hang-ups" to avoid being prejudiced or judgmental; otherwise he may be treating himself rather than the patient.

In psychosomatic medicine the objective of psychotherapy is to improve the patient's physical symptoms or to cure them completely but it is likely that success also implies that the patient acquires an improved awareness of his own potential and enjoys a more relaxed and interesting life. After a gap of fifteen years I met a man whose asthma had been treated by psychotherapy. I asked him, "How is the asthma?" and he replied, "I don't have asthma, but what I do have is that when I speak at board meetings people listen to me now".

To achieve this objective the therapist must allow the patient to become aware of the reasons why he has become ill. The reasons are almost always concerned with how we feel, rather than what we think, about our life and relationships. At school we are taught to write and count and maybe to think but few people have had an opportunity or encouragement to learn how to cope with feelings of anger, grief, guilt or even happiness.

The problem is complicated by the fact that the reasons are usually obscure, are unconscious or are totally forgotten and are certainly not seen as relevant to the current illness. They must somehow be brought into the light of day and of consciousness. In this process it is vital that the patient should appear to make the discovery for himself, since we really only accept advice we give ourselves.

This is obviously a matter of technique which can be learned so as to avoid direct interpretations. I often feel the therapist's role is like that of a sheep dog who knows when to sit down on the grass and wait, and knows when to cut off diversionary escape routes, and knows when to yap at the heels so that his charges can decide to move safely through the gate to new pastures.

The patient must be allowed to tell the story in his own way and at his own pace while the therapist may rearrange it in his own head to suit his own habits and needs. He must clarify the chronology and the impact of the events asking himself the while, "Why did he take ill when he did?" As we listen we note important aspects of the story such as previous personal and family illness, age of parents, brothers, sisters and offspring and particularly the approximate dates of bereavements and equivalent events. Births, deaths and marriages are common trigger points of illness. Aspects of the patient's personality and those of the spouse become apparent, as do interests, hobbies, aims and mood.

The opportunity to offload the whole story is in itself therapeutic. This has been called catharsis and indeed often is a symbolic chance for the patient to verbalise and "excrete" his feelings of guilt, inadequacy and loss of confidence. The patient must be encouraged to continue talking in subsequent meetings and will begin to see his problems more clearly once they have been expressed in words. He can then decide his priorities to deal with the most important problems first. It is rather like a hiker who has to re-pack his rucksack so that the load is less uncomfortable to carry.

Inevitably some of the communication is non-verbal and therapists gifted with acute powers of observation are tuned to notice topics which induce in their patient tension, anger or sadness. The lady who sits uneasily in her chair constantly twisting or removing her wedding ring seems genuinely surprised if you ask gently if she feels her marriage is in peril.

At the auditory level many phrases used have double meanings as if the patient were testing you out to see if you will explore a sensitive area, yet will not lose face if you miss the clue or ignore it. A phrase like "things get on top of me" is an obvious example but it may be that a word is used slightly out of context or is an apparent slip of the tongue. These words or phrases are usually highly charged with significance for the patient.

"And is there any other illness in your family?"

"Nothing worth talking about."

"And what is it you don't wish to talk about?"

"My brother is in a psychiatric hospital."

or

"And how is your mother?"

"She's not very nice. I mean not very well!"

This type of listening is helping the therapist to act as a catalyst by allowing the patient to become aware of things which are barely conscious. To explore the hidden dimensions of the illness may require other methods. Many patients have written short stories, or poetry; while some have brought paintings or drawings. These activities may be helpful in offering clues. It is sometimes worth asking the patient to draw his illness and certainly the doodles done while speaking on the telephone or during committee meetings are invaluable, especially as they are almost always done without any conscious thought.

Another useful area of non-verbal communication is to note the choice of reading matter on the bedside table. One lady who claimed her home life was idyllic was reading a book entitled "Two is Lonely". My staff, inevitably, teased me about this eccentricity, one house physician saying, "A very ill lady has been admitted, but you will be relieved to hear she is reading a book called "The Survivor"!

Patients' gifts are often a message. One lady, whom I suspected of having a drink problem, mainly by reason of what she did not say, had strong denial defences. One day as she left I asked her, "Are you sure there isn't something else you had to tell me?" On her next visit she presented me with a bottle of whisky. A useful "opener" in both senses!

For me the royal road to the hidden unconscious is through dreams. If the patient is prepared to note his dreams it is surprising how much he is helped in the psychotherapeutic process. Dreams tend to produce symbolic pictures and stories to describe feelings which are difficult to express in words and the attempt may destroy the feeling - it is like reducing a magnificent sunset to an analysis of the wave lengths of light. Often we can allow the symbolism of dreams to help.

If dreams are offered they should be shared and discussed since it is only the patient's view of the dream message which is of relevance. At first the therapist may offer his ideas on the symbolism of the dream, emphasising that he is only using his impressions rather as an architect will offer alternative plans for a building but allow the client to choose which design is appropriate for his present need. Before long and with some encouragement the patient will offer his own ideas on his dreams.

Much has been published on the interpretation of dreams but it is likely that the standard interpretations are of limited help since they are seldom related to the actual life situation under consideration and should only be used as suggestions and guide lines. I personally gained most help from J A Hadfield's book **Dreams and Nightmares** (17)

In the early stages of therapy I feel it is important to identify and enlarge upon the positive aspects of dreams such as movement, sunshine and exploration rather than the negative messages of violence, sexual difficulties and so on. These will be explored in their own good time.

I can recall many years ago, admitting a patient for an incidental physical disease (who was undergoing a Freudian analysis). She complained of insomnia and said to me, "If only I didn't have that awful nightmare". I was caught between the requirement that I should not interfere in the work she was doing with her analyst and a mixture of curiosity and a wish to help her sleep. So I asked about the nightmare and she replied, "Every night I am threatening my children with an umbrella; it's phallic and I'm being male and not a mother". I said, "But look, you have a choice, it is an umbrella and if you open it, it is a sheltering symbol of mothering and femininity". The nightmare ceased.

Hadfield has pointed out that nightmares and recurring dreams often delineate the problem which has to be solved and the nightmare is often followed by dreams which offer alternative ways of dealing with the problem. Certainly we cannot dream in capital letters or italics, so we tend to have horrific dreams that compel us to pay attention. Some dreams appear to be mainly of immediate help, as in dreams which plan the next day's shopping list or menu. This is the manifest or obvious message but most dreams also have a latent emotional message. It has been suggested that the type of dream offered depends on the training and expectation of the therapist and that Jungian dreams are only offered to Jungian trained psychotherapists. This seems to me to be a nonsense.

In my experience dreams reflect aspects of the patient's character and creativity. Practical people tend to have quite obvious practical dreams which are fairly easy to understand. Those with the capacity for story telling dream up splendid plots for fiction writing and will continue to use this gift after they have solved their medical problems. Those lucky people who possess the gift of poetry produce dreams of arresting beauty and quite outstanding artistry.

The characters we produce in our dreams may often be chosen from casual encounters of the day, though we may appear in different and multiple disguises in one dream. We appear as our benevolent or malevolent self, as the opposite sex, as a child and so on. Time clues in dreams are often provided in the background. Dreams describing feelings in earlier life may underline the time scale by steam trains, school bags or long lost fashion in clothing, somewhere in the background.

People who tend to be intellectual and have been pushed by ambitious parents often dream of flying, high buildings or in the sky colours of blue and white; while those who are surer of their own emotional value tend to dream of gardens and swimming and in earthy colours of brown or green.

Dreams certainly have a sense of humour and tend to make puns and jokes and indeed to make mock of the dreamer. The dream of doing a crossword puzzle often indicates that we have been having "cross words" with someone. Actual physical changes may be signposted in dreams - if there is a dream of the house being flooded it is always wise to check for swollen ankles from water retention.

It is interesting to watch lateralisation in dreams since right is our dexterous side while the sinister left is much more emotional in content. The classical dream of a road with offices, factories and libraries on the right and with gardens, woodlands and sun soaked beaches on the left is offering the dreamer a choice. Some dreams may offer different meanings for the sexes. The tooth is a primitive symbol of attack and defence and may indicate aggressive power. The female losing a tooth in her dream is often becoming more feminine and warm, while the male may be losing his drive and potency either professionally, emotionally or physically.

In the course of psychotherapy the patient will often resolve long hidden problems and resentments from earlier life by using the therapist as the problem-relative and solving the old dilemma in the process. This is part of the phenomenon known as transference. It is the vital key to successful therapy and deserves its own chapter.

Perhaps the most rewarding part of psychotherapeutic process is that it is often like throwing a stone into a pool of water. The ripples spread out and in his turn the former patient helps those whom he encounters in later life. This valuable by-product is seen to advantage in teachers, medical and nursing personnel and in other caring professions, but almost magical help can sometimes be offered by former patients over the garden wall or in chance encounters in train or bus. Many ex-patients have themselves become counsellors or psychotherapists and my most enduring reward is to see former patients demonstrating skill and success far superior to that of their erstwhile mentor.

If we accept that the psychosomatic approach is at least worthy of consideration, the doctor's first and most important task is to be careful. He or she must be careful not to overlook the early stages of serious organic disease or of less serious conditions which are readily treatable by medication or surgery. If a recognised psychosomatic disorder is apparent, or if the story is obscure and confused, we have to assess whether psychological help would be appropriate.

The general practitioner or the hospital physician is in an advantageous position. He sees large numbers of patients and can select those who might benefit from a psychotherapeutic intervention. He has no need to refer them further and indeed can have them working hard at their problems without the idea of psychotherapy ever being discussed. He can comfort himself regarding those he has considered as unsuitable for psychotherapy with the cynical thought that they are no worse off than they would be with a totally "organic" medical adviser.

It is important to develop some intuition as to which patients are suitable for psychotherapy not only because psychotherapeutic time is a fairly unusual and expensive resource but also because we undoubtedly have the potential to make some patients worse rather than better. Indeed, there are some patients whose illness is their only social asset and who might well be lost without it. It is therefore important for the doctor to decide fairly promptly if the patient is clearly unsuitable for any type of psychotherapy. Doctors should regard psychotherapy as an adjunct to the treatment plan and use medication, surgery etc. when and where they are required. The objective is a healthy patient and no holds barred to achieve success.

During the process of selection it is wise for the doctor to make some kind of early assessment of what outcome is expected. Do we hope to cure, to relieve or merely to support the patient? An even more sinister pitfall is that we may feel inadequate and guilty and project our unconscious anger and frustration on to the patient by referring him for unnecessary surgery or other "punitive" procedures. In selecting patients we have to consider both the illness and the patient.

The Illness The commonly accepted psychosomatic diseases seem to benefit from a psychotherapeutic approach. It is perhaps more doubtful if we can help true hypertension and other illnesses which have already passed the point of no return before being diagnosed. Illnesses of short duration and of considerable severity respond well. Acute vomiting, severe headache and explosive ulcerative colitis are surprisingly amenable to treatment.

The Patient The patients' suitability seems to rest on their motivation to get well; on their ability to communicate and on their "ego-strength" and insight. The well-motivated patient

has no secondary gain from the illness and is felt to be capable
of change in attitude or even to admit that he might on
occasion be wrong! The rigid individual who has never has a
change of occupation or employer is likely to prove an uphill
task.

It is important that the patient should be able to communicate
even at the first interview and this skill will improve. It has
been said that psychotherapy is impossible with the deaf as
they cannot communicate but I have found that with really
expert help from hearing aid specialists, reliable
communication can be achieved, especially if the doctor can
be motivated to learn some sign language. The knowledge so
gained of the deaf person's life and difficulties is both
rewarding and humbling. Access to non-verbal
communication with patients who paint, doodle, write or
dream is clearly advantageous.
"Ego-strength" is rather a jargon word but it is a useful
assessment of constitutional strength and yet also implies a
capacity to bend rather than to break. Highly rigid
personalities are often too brittle to cope with psychotherapy
as unpleasant creatures may crawl out as we we lift up or
move the stones in their defences. Patients who are sceptical
and slightly aggressive are still "in the game" and often do
well, while "yes-men" who tend to agree with everything are
often difficult to help. The patient's normal tolerance of
alcohol or medication may be a useful guide to "ego-strength".
A reasonable track record of achievement and of coping with
previous mishaps is some guide to the character requirement.
A sense of humour is a massive asset for therapy as cure often
equates with a capacity to laugh at ourselves and life.

Insight is difficult to measure in the early stages. My
undergraduates often enquire why I ask patients whether they
preferred English or Mathematics at school. I find that
mathematicians are very logical thinkers and have difficulty
in lateral thinking, which is needed to see associations and
connections in their statements, symptoms and behaviour.

They may therefore be more difficult psychotherapeutic subjects than patients who enjoy literature, history and the vagaries of humanity. Intelligence, as distinct from intellectuality, is a help but I am sceptical as to whether social class or previous educational achievement are factors in acquiring self-awareness and insight.

In the first few interviews it should be possible for the doctor to form some estimate of the patients' emotional and developmental maturity, of their aims and outlook and of their awareness and acceptance of their own sexual identity.

It may help our assessment to do some direct questioning in the early stages and we all acquire our favourite questions - When did you last feel perfectly well? If you were cured tomorrow, what would you most like to do that you cannot do at present? Do you ever get angry? When were you most frightened in your whole life? "What is the worst thing that you have ever done? If you have evening visitors, can you leave the dishes unwashed until next morning?

I try to decide whether psychotherapy is worth pursuing in the first few interviews and before a dependent relationship develops. Undoubtedly during this time, assessment is a two-way process. If the therapist is vaguely aware that the patient is non-cooperative yet is good therapeutic material, it may be that the "faces don't fit". Another therapist may therefore be successful and this offer is often accepted. Patients with a difficult father may initially feel threatened by a male therapist and a change to a female may be of help. Clearly they will have to deal with their relationship to the father eventually but it may pay dividends to circumnavigate this problem in the early stages. In my hospital practice I was privileged to have a series of highly gifted social workers and trainees who fulfiled this role of "alternative therapists".

It is interesting how often the patient is late for the third meeting. By then he has to decide whether to trust the therapist and tell the rest of the story or to plan his escape route. He may, of course, default and have been "scared into health".

If the patient and therapist appear to be mutually compatible after the first few interviews, I tend to offer an open-ended contract that we will meet and talk for three months. We can than reassess the situation as to whether we are wasting one another's time or whether we should continue and finish our task.

7. Transference

In Nature's infinite book of secrecy,
A little I can read.

William Shakespeare

Transference is defined in the dictionary as the act of transferring from one person or place to another. The psychological idea of transference is perhaps closer to the "transfers" we played with in childhood but is the key to a great deal of human action.

Whenever two people meet there is an obvious manifest transaction, if only that of buying a newspaper, but at the same time there may be a latent feeling of pleasure or uneasiness which is not of obvious cause. Many years ago I registered a feeling of oppression whenever I visited my tobacconist, before the days when buying tobacco was calculated to induce guilt feelings! So one day I sat down for an hour and worked on it. I gradually became aware that the tobacconist physically resembled someone who had bullied me at school. Thereafter we became good friends and to my surprise I discovered that we had attended the same school albeit with a twenty year gap in ages! This capacity to project feelings or characteristics onto other people is an unconscious process and the particular transference is vital to the role of doctors or counsellors; especially as they often receive feelings transferred from earlier life onto a present and probably inappropriate situation.

The mechanism of transference is largely one of projection, a psychological device which must be clearly understood. To some extent we all tend to behave like cinema projectors and throw onto the screen parts of our personality, our past and our character without which we would feel much better people. It is indeed a silver screen as we usually direct our projections onto people we trust or would like to trust. If we are not constantly aware of projection and are on the receiving end we become confused by the inappropriate messages. The young husband who is constantly accused of extravagance should perhaps explore his wife's past history and may find that her father or even her grandfather had the misfortune to be declared bankrupt.

If we fail to recognise that the message is a projection, we may well be missing a vital piece of the clinical jigsaw puzzle, but more importantly, we may be entangled in the trap of projective identification. This is where we accept the inappropriate labels and accusations as partly true and react accordingly. If a patient constantly implies that he is no better and that the counsellor is not giving adequate help, there is some danger of identifying with this projection and the counsellor can soon run out of ideas on how to help the patient. If we recognise the projection, we can suggest that it might just be possible that he is describing his own feelings of inadequacy and helplessness.

The new patient often arrives in a state of apprehension as to the consultation and its outcome, so he has to regard his doctor as all-powerful and wise. He needs omnipotence at this stage. Most of us would wish to deny such strength but it is needed as a temporary fantasy by the patient. It is no good trying to show understanding by saying, "I know, I've had a slipped disc too." The patient wants an infallible doctor and is angry at not being unique in his suffering and certainly does not wish to be treated by a physician who cannot cure himself! So at this point in the transference; the helper is expected to be an omnipotent deity. Sadly, some consultants accept this identification and believe it to be true, often with disastrous results.

As we establish a good working rapport the transference changes and the counsellor can be accepted as less than god-like. We become a series of people important in the patient's life or expectations and must constantly assess who we are thought to be, as we will be used in that role to work through unresolved problems from the past. The common roles we play are the omnipotent doctor, an authority figure who judges, a parent, sibling, spouse, fiancee or child. It is interesting that this occurs regardless of the age or sex of the helper. A young man under training in his twenties takes some time to get used to being seen as a mother! All these roles may be either positive or negative and we quickly learn to pick up clues and to spot a change of role.
If, for example, the patient says, "You are patronising me" he is clearly in the negative transference state and we might ask for more information about the real father or, perhaps, if the relationship is robust, say, "But I'm not your father".

It is always interesting to find one is being treated as the child when, for instance, the patient says, "You are sitting in a draught". If the transference is negative the message is, "I hope you catch pneumonia and stop stirring up my feelings". If there is a positive relationship the message is, "I would like to help and take care of you". This is often an opportunity to be reasonably directive as the patient may be willing to change his outlook or to make a decision to please "the child".

In the training and supervision of young therapists it helps to ask them to make a note of the transference role and its polarity at the end of each session until it becomes an automatic observation.

Clearly we have to accept a lot of anger from some patients and this is easier if we realise it is not personal animosity. Probably the most difficult transference to cope with is when we are placed in the boyfriend/girlfriend role. The feeling is quite intense and if we do not understand the transference phenomenon it would be easy to imagine that this was a real love affair. That, sadly, is how genuinely caring people may find themselves in deep trouble, especially if the positive affection suddenly switches to negative vengeance. When in doubt we must interpret and explain the transference mechanism.

The situation is complicated by the same mechanism, at work in the therapist, called counter transference. Again it may either be positive or negative. If it is over-positive we see all our geese as swans and tend to be manipulated, while if it is strongly negative we may need, unconsciously, to punish the patient if only by suggesting yet another physical investigation. It often helps to discuss the situation with a trusted colleague.

If the patient is talking to you and also to his priest, social worker or anyone else, there may be a dilution and splitting of the transference with resultant confusion. All progress stops. It helps to decide which member of the team has the transference rapport and the others should remain uninvolved as far as possible. Well-orientated family doctors usually indicate the role they want their consultants to adopt. It has been my privilege to work with many unusually sensitive and skilled family doctors who are able to indicate the attitude most helpful for their patients. In one week I had two referrals from the same general practitioner - the first letter stated, "Could you spend some time with this patient. I shall be happy to cope with prescriptions and similar transactions". The second letter said, "I have a good relationship with this patient and his problems. I should be glad to have an electrocardiogram and an assessment of his cardiovascular state".

The Freudian analysts hope, I suspect, to avoid or diminish transference problems by sitting out of sight at the end of the couch. There is no such escape clause for those interested in psychosomatic medicine since occasions arise in the course of a mainly psychotherapeutic relationship when it is necessary to re-examine a patient to check progress or to look for complications. When this situation arises it is vitally necessary to assess the transference state since it is obvious that physical examination may be construed as either seduction or assault depending on whether the transference is positive or negative. If the physical examination is not urgent it is wise to spend a session discussing the need for the check up and the feelings it may induce and to ask permission to be a "stethoscope doctor" at the next visit.

If a sudden crisis develops, as when you suspect a patient with ulcerative colitis may have developed a rectal abscess, it may be wiser to ask a colleague to carry out the examination. Otherwise you may have to spend the next few weeks or months sorting out the patient's homosexual or heterosexual fantasies.

I remember with retrospective amusement being asked to visit an outlying psychiatric hospital as a matter of some urgency. I set off after the normal day's work to drive ninety dark and hazardous miles through a January snow storm. I was greeted on the doorstep of the hospital by a psychiatrist who said, "You were the only physician I could think of who would understand if I said I couldn't possibly do a rectal examination on this patient!"

There are, of course, occasions when touch is permissible and necessary, as with the terminally ill and indeed, in bereavement, a "non-sexual" hug may well be life-saving.

The transference phenomenon gives the helpers tremendous power over the helped and since we are in a position of trust it also gives us immense responsibilities. It is deplorable that some often pseudo-religious groups seem prepared to invoke and exploit the transference to wield power and to extract money from their followers. The truly caring professionals must understand and use the transference mechanism with humility, sensitivity and tenderness.

8. Symbolic disorders

It would not be at all a bad thing if the elite of the medical world be a little less clever and adopt a more primitive method of thinking and reason more as children do.

Georg Groddek

Many years ago I was telephoned by an Ear, Nose and Throat surgeon who had admitted a man in his twenties for a minor nose operation and asked if I could see the patient as he was vomiting two or three times a day and the vomiting had started on the day after his marriage some six months previously. Clearly a very unusual and insightful surgeon! My visit to the patient confirmed the story but no further information was proffered.

I asked if his wife had been pregnant before the marriage and this he acknowledged. "So", I asked, "you have wondered if you would have married her had this not been the case?" He agreed. After some further talk I suggested that I would visit him the next day and asked if he would try to remember any dream he might have that night.

When I returned the following afternoon the vomiting had stopped. He said, "That was a funny thing you asked me to do yesterday. I dreamt that my wife had died and that I married her twin sister. But she hasn't got a twin sister". He was able to appreciate that his dream emphasised that he would have married the lady anyway and his feelings of rejection of her ceased

Rejection is such an early and powerful feeling for most people and the symbolic disorders relating to it are very common. I think it is important to appreciate that it would have been quite unrewarding to try to reassure this man at an intellectual level. Dreams have a quality equivalent to real emotional experience which allows acceptance, reassurance and change of behaviour to occur. It is unusual to have such instant relief of symptoms, though it is more likely in acute conditions and I am fairly sure that family doctors frequently achieve this type of success.

Another and similarly remarkable example may underline this mechanism. An obstetrician telephoned to say he had a patient with severe pregnancy vomiting and he proposed to take her off intravenous therapy if I could see her at once. I set off for the maternity hospital and was somewhat concerned to discover that the patient, in her first pregnancy, was herself an obstetrician and was not a little embarrassed by her difficult pregnancy.

As we talked, it became evident that the lady was unconsciously rejecting the baby and was doing so as she was rejecting her own femininity. She was convinced that she would be unable to cope with the demands of motherhood. Both her father and grandfather were medical men and she identified herself with medicine and this as an almost exclusively male role. She had been brought up by nursemaids and seldom saw her mother who appeared to be a bit of a socialite. Clearly she had had little opportunity of acquiring a female mothering identity.

Again I asked her to record her dreams and returned to see her the following morning. Her one dream was that she had gone back to her original home and had gone straight to her mother's bedroom. She hunted through the wardrobes until she found her mother's most expensive and glamorous gown and this she put on. This dream so clearly showed that she was now able to identify with her mother and was reassured as to her femininity and her capacity for motherhood. Her pregnancy proceeded uneventfully.

Another demonstration of the message which may be conveyed by physical symptoms was a forty-five-year-old lady referred by a surgeon. She had been admitted as a possible high intestinal obstruction but no explanation for her epigastric pain and continual vomiting had been discovered. My initial interview revealed no recent stress but I noted that her father had died when she was seven years of age. She denied being a dreamer but was interested in drawing and painting so I asked her to draw a picture of her illness.

At my next visit she offered her drawing. It showed a female figure formed of coiled spirals for the limbs, and the upper abdomen was aggressively transfixed by two arrows. My association was that the limbs, drawn as coiled springs, might be a pun on "in spring a young man's fancy ...." so I suggested that the arrows might be Cupid's darts. This produced a bout of weeping and she described her fears of her husband's infidelity. It may have been she felt that it was some evil quality in her which caused father and perhaps her husband to forsake her and it was probably this that she was trying to eliminate by her vomiting.

Other bodily areas and functions may be used in this type of symbolic disorder. For example I recall a fifty year old married civil engineer who was referred with a short history of typical anginal pain. Extensive investigations failed to reveal my heart disease or hyperlipidaemia. He was a very successful, if slightly ruthless, man with a branch of his business in Germany. I felt that mere reassurance would not be adequate to relieve his symptoms so I suggested that he had a "heart ache" and wondered if there was "an affair of the heart" somewhere around.

It transpired that his partner in Germany had died recently of a heart attack so there was an element of identification in his illness. He had gone to help clear up some problems in the German office and had fallen in love with his late partner's daughter who was in her mid-twenties. We discussed the situation and I enquired if he was really prepared to embark on a further round of child rearing with all its demands and responsibilities, as the lady was clearly entitled to have a family.

I also suggested gently that at this stage she might really be looking for a father rather than a husband and hinted at the likely possibility of sexual difficulties as a result of this understandable confusion of her needs.

Again the logical approach would require some emotional confirmation so I arranged a further appointment and suggested he might try to note any dreams, a request greeted with some scepticism. On his return visit he had been free of pain and proffered one dream that he said was totally irrelevant to his problem. He had dreamt he had decided to buy a new car and chose a Mercedes sports model. As he was writing the cheque he decided he liked his old car better! Totally irrelevant?

The permutations are endless in this type of symbolic illness and one keeps meeting new examples. A patient with back pain was referred after full orthopaedic investigations had proved negative, and almost in her first sentence she said, "Actually I'm scared stiff".

It is, of course, absolutely essential to avoid the pitfall of adopting symbolic interpretation too freely or too slickly. It is vital for all possible organic disorders to be considered before even contemplating a symbolic explanation. On the other hand it is equally irresponsible to overlook an emotional cause when such a discovery can achieve permanent benefit for the patient.

9. Water retention syndrome

Home they brought her warrior dead;
She nor swoon'd nor utter'd cry,
All her maidens, watching, said
"She must weep or she will die".

Lord Tennyson

Water retention syndromes offer an interesting challenge to the psychosomatic approach, since they vary from cases of gross oedema, which are undoubtedly organic in nature, to cases which have long been recognised as having some psychological basis. The organic oedemas are seen in congestive cardiac failure, renal disease, the hypoproteinaemias and in carcinomas which secrete anti-diuretic hormone.

Clearly the physician must first eliminate the organic causes but one finds that there are still a number of patients who have water retention which cannot be explained by these mechanisms. In addition to more or less continuous oedema there are a number of transient intermittent oedemas which have been called periodic oedema, of which angioneurotic oedema is an example.

Angio-oedema was first described by Robert Graves (18), of thyroid fame, in 1843 though it was more carefully studied by Heinrich Quincke (19) in 1882 who drew attention to its resemblance to "the frequent menstrual oedemas".

A great deal of published work is available on normal and abnormal water metabolism, and it is characterised by confusing and contradictory statements partly, I suspect, because the emotional factors tend to be ignored. In the standard works, only De Wardener (20) appears to note that stress may produce either diuresis or anti-diuresis.

There is, of course, a known association between water retention and familial or potential diabetes mellitus, and such patients often respond to diabetic dietary regimes. The more modern researchers have been interested in the genetic component. (Frank et al. (21) Ballogh et al. (22). Treatment has been suggested for recurrent oedema by using plasmin inhibitors such as methyl-testosterone or danazol to increase the Cl esterase inhibitor.

So we arrive at last at the emotional factors. With hindsight I found that in 1956 Schottstaedt, Grace and Wolff (23) had reported that "stimuli perceived as hazardous were accompanied by restrained behaviour, feelings of increased alertness and retention of water and sodium, whereas sudden release from such threats was associated with water diuresis".

My own interest in the condition began in the early 1960s by a strange process of chance. One afternoon at my outpatient medical clinic at a peripheral hospital I saw an elderly woman with typical angio-oedema with swelling of the upper lip and both orbits. When I explored her life situation at the onset, the story unfolded that she had been asked to visit a sister who was a patient in hospital. As she was on poor terms with this sister she did not bother to go and visit. She discovered shortly afterwards that this had been a deathbed request and her feelings of bereavement were complicated by feelings of guilt. She said that she had not wept as she "was not given to crying" and within hours had developed swelling of her eyelids and face.

On my way back to Glasgow after the clinic I had to see a patient in the local Maternity Hospital who had developed rapidly increasing oedema. She had been seen on the previous day by my consultant colleague, but her condition was deteriorating, so the physicians were recalled. I knew that my colleague would have excluded renal or cardiac disease or pre-eclamptic toxaemia, so I could only try listening! The patient was having her first baby and eventually she told me that she had just had a letter that her mother had died in the Outer Hebrides and that her father had summoned her to come and help in the domestic crisis. Knowing the power of the West Highland father I became equally authoritative and indicated that her responsibility was to her child, and that someone else could go and help her father. The next day the hospital telephoned to ask what treatment I had prescribed as the patient had had a massive diuresis, had lost 3.5 Kilos in weight and was almost free of oedema.

For good measure, when I reached my main hospital the next morning I found we had admitted a 38-year-old actor from one of the local theatres whose face was swollen to the dimensions of a football. He was a very minor actor in the show and I could find no deaths among his friends or relatives. He denied any bereavement, but then said, "It depends what you mean by bereavement". Apparently he was extremely found of the leading lady of the company but had refused to propose to her as her income was four times his own. On the day before his admission she had declared that she could wait no longer and would find another potential husband. Again the diuresis was rapid and we had an engagement party!

As usually happens when one stumbles upon a finding such as this, further cases appear to add anecdotal if not statistical evidence and the challenge to find scientific proof is as tantalising as it is elusive.

In an attempt to avoid observer error my colleague Dr Ian Glen recalled, for interview, patients who had attended the Dermatology Clinic, suffering from angio-oedema, in the previous three years. He collected 30 patients and we had 20 from our own unit. Of these 50, 46 (92%) showed a bereavement or separation situation and 39 (78%) had associated guilt, anger or resentment. The one feature which occurred in almost every case was that the patients said they had been discouraged from showing feelings, and especially from weeping, in their childhood. The clinical picture seems to represent the body language of suppressed weeping with the swollen eyes and the "stiff upper lip".

Dr Glen and I felt we might have a psychosomatic disorder which could be measured (24). We examined a large series of water-retainers and ended up with 55 patients and we used 21 lab. workers and medical students as controls. The water retention patients had a significantly lower solute output for the same urine flow compared to the controls (p = 0.01). A psychotherapeutic interview tended to increase the solute output and to reduce this difference from the control in the two hours following interview, though not to statistical significance (25).

One of the difficulties encountered in this research was in trying to organise a control period with the minimum of

ommunication since even a kind word from the staff resulted
n a massive and rapid diuresis. Clearly, sophisticated
psychotherapy was seldom required and many "cures"
followed one interview.

On the whole we confirmed the findings of previous workers
that situations of stress involving anger, defence and
resentment in which the patients tended to withdraw seemed
to produce oliguria, while relaxed and reassuring attitudes
with easy communication produced an outgoing situation
symbolic even in terms of urinary outflow. It seems likely
that ordinary healthy people have these responses also, but do
not react with the violent fluctuations which characterise
patients with water retention syndromes.

To check if a situation of reality stress could produce this type
of change we did our standard collections on a man having an
endoscopy for peptic ulcer. During the hour preceding the
endoscopy and during it, urinary output fell to 3 mls per hour
and rapidly returned to normal after the procedure was
completed.

Another patient with chronic water retention reached hospital
for the tests and became involved in a heated argument with
the staff who had not been warned of her arrival. During the
control period of urine collections she became even more
furious and resentful and her urinary output fell to 2.7 mls
per hour. Thereafter she had her interview which was
somewhat aggressive but reasonably cathartic and her urinary
output rose to 148 mls per hour thereafter.

I have traced detailed records of 68 patients with water
retention syndromes comprising 55 females and 13 males with
an age range from 21 to 57 (average 41) years. 43 had angio-
oedema and 25 had periodic oedema. 42 patients required
only one interview and 26 had psychotherapy for times
varying from one month to four years. The special features
noted were that 57 (84%) had experienced "bereavement" in

its widest sense and in 28 (41%) this was associated with strong feelings of guilt. Of the 68 patients only 6 admitted that they could weep easily and without embarrassment. It is likely that water retention syndromes are common in the United Kingdom and perhaps especially in Scotland where children, particularly boys, are strongly discouraged from showing emotion and are mocked if they weep. The ultimate term of derision in primary schools is "cry baby'"

The case histories noted earlier are fairly typical and demonstrate how rapidly many patients respond to the most ordinary opportunity for sympathetic listening. Certainly many are quite dramatic in their response. One elderly lady with quite gross oedema attended an outpatient clinic, and when no obvious reason for her fluid retention was found, her immediate family history was scrutinised and she reported that her husband was dying of cancer in a surgical ward at the hospital. While we discussed this sad tale she asked if she might be excused to empty her bladder so we measured the volume which proved to be over a litre.

A more complex problem was that of a 48-year-old lady who attended the hospital with typical angio-oedema. She had a three years history of recurring oedema and three months before I saw her had been admitted to another hospital with genuine intestinal obstruction requiring a resection of small bowel. To the astonishment of the surgeon and pathologist the occlusion was entirely due to interstitial oedema of the bowel wall (26). The story of events at the onset of her illness was that she was caught in a state of indecision as her mother was seriously ill in Edinburgh and her daughter was in labour with her first child in Glasgow. The patient decided to stand by her daughter and her mother died. She couldn't weep or express her guilt feelings as her only memory of her mother was of her saying, "Big girls don't cry". She was encouraged to weep and diuresis followed.

The sequel to this story was that I had an urgent telephone

call at the hospital one morning some three months later. The woman sounded husky, breathless and distressed and I feared that she was developing laryngeal oedema. I hastily collected a supply of "water-pills" and drove some five miles across the city to her home. She opened her door saying, "Immediately I spoke to you by telephone I began to improve and I'm now quite comfortable". It transpired that her ten year old nephew had died. She subsequently reported that at the nephew's funeral the officiating clergyman had said to the child's mother, "Now, you mustn't cry". My patient had seized the astonished parson by the shoulder and said, "Never, ever say that again!"

I shall conclude this topic with two purely speculative suggestions in the hope that others may in the future throw light on the ideas.

At a clinical conference I saw a middle aged woman who had rheumatoid arthritis and Sjogren's Syndrome with dry uncomfortable eyes as her main complaint. She had slightly swollen ankles and it occurred to me that the dry eyes might also be a symbolic message about weeping and tears. I asked her if she had been allowed to cry as a child and she gave this splendid and illuminating reply, "Oh no, I was never allowed to cry and I cannot relieve myself".

My second speculation is that there may be a link between the emotional aspects of water retention syndromes and that of nephrosis. I have seen this apparently occur on two occasions and offer one case history as potential evidence.

A 16 year old youth was admitted with generalised oedema, gross albuminuria, low serum albumen and high cholesterol. By sheer luck he passed his time in hospital drawing sketches. His first was of a boy with a shock of fuzzy hair in a hospital bed. The second was an identical boy in the dock in court being judged by a rather stern looking man. Clearly there was a story and it slowly unfolded.

At the age of seven the patient had been sent on holiday to an aunt who lived in Scotland. When his parents were due to rejoin the boy they failed to appear and had, in fact, separated. After their divorce he was in his mother's custody and had been in boarding school in England. He only re-met his father some six weeks before his admission and the father had taken him on holiday and had then sent him back to his aunt in Scotland. The patient clearly felt he was on trial by his father and the repeat journey to the aunt seemed not only to reawaken the earlier trauma but convinced him that he had failed the test of acceptability. It is interesting that within three weeks he had a normal urine and a return of all his biochemical parameters to conventional levels.

To summarise - we are as yet ignorant of the exact metabolic pathways that lead to water retention but in psychotherapy we have a powerful and effective tool to help recovery in many patients. A typical patient will have been brought up to repress grief and to avoid weeping. The symptoms arise in situations of bereavement often associated with guilt.

10. Externalised disorders

Not learning more than the fond eye doth teach;
Which pries not to the interior, but, like the martlets,
Builds in the weather on the outward wall,
Even in the force and road of casualty.

William Shakespeare

To some extent we can all externalise our feelings. We blush or go pale, we perspire or we become rigid, even rooted to the spot. It is possible that an exaggeration of such mechanisms may proceed to actual physical lesions. In dermatology it has been suggested that the distribution of a rash may in itself be symbolic with observations that individuals who have to fend off threats develop rashes affecting outer surfaces as in psoriasis, while the child who needs to cling develops eczema on the inner arms if denied this need.

I saw a hospital outpatient with fairly typical gall-bladder dyspepsia who was of normal appearance at the first interview. To my surprise when she was undressed for the physical examination she was covered by a skin rash which stopped at wrists, mid-thighs, and in a "V" at her neck line so that no rash was normally visible. My curiosity was aroused and I took more of her story without finding any stress factor. The necessary x-rays and other investigations were organised and as she left I remarked that I was cynical enough to think that she might have a problem, but that she needed to put a good face on it for the sake of public appearances. On her return visit she admitted to having an alcoholic husband and had found her skin much less troublesome since she had herself realised the association.

Many years ago I was asked to see a patient in the hospital dermatology department. He was a thirty-eight year old teacher who had been an in-patient for three months with severe and painful erythromelalgia (heat and pain) of both arms, and no treatment had been of any help. He was a rather austere academic who was lying in bed in a cold room with fans and iced water sprays playing on his suspended arms. He was articulate and highly intelligent. When asked about his childhood he said that he only played on rooftops, and admitted that if his wife asked him to pull a lettuce from their garden he had to wear gloves. It seemed likely that this reluctance to become involved in anything earthy would extend to his marriage so I asked if he had any children. Apparently his wife had presented an ultimatum and had insisted on adopting a child. They now had a five months old adopted child and the rash had started when his wife had asked him to pick up a soiled nappy. As I was at that time only embarking on my training in psychotherapy I referred him to a psychoanalyst colleague who rapidly produced a successful outcome.

The skin is so accessible that it is more than usually prone to self-inflicted wounds of which I shall quote two examples.
A gynaecologist renowned for his intuition requested the transfer to our medical ward of a middle aged lady. She had for years complained of ulceration of the vulva. At her initial

interview I discovered that she was widowed fairly recently and also that she did not remember her own father as her mother became a widow while the patient was in her infancy. She had six older brothers. I asked about the mother and was told that she was very strict and very religious, in a somewhat Calvinistic fashion. The patient said that her mother was always first up and about in the household. When the morning paper was delivered she scanned it and tore out all the pictures of females before her sons could see them. So I remarked, "And could it be that you too have to tear away your feminity". The lesions healed rapidly and did not recur.

The second example was recounted to me by a very forthright family doctor. He had written to a headmistress regarding one of his young patients who was constantly scratching her face and he asked if she could be encouraged to wear gloves in class. He received a reply to the effect that he would, of course, remember that tearing the face was a very ancient sign of mourning. The pupil's elder sister had died of leukaemia but the younger child only knew that her sister had gone to hospital and had never returned. The headmistress suggested that an explanation of her sister's death might be more effective than humiliation before her classmates.

Body image at its most literal level is often a factor, and frequently a distorted factor, in the overweight and the underweight patient. In both states the underlying causation is invariably complex and confusing and one must avoid the pitfall of generalisation as no clear pattern of cause and effect is tenable. The organic causes of weight loss or excessive weight gain are fortunately fairly easy to diagnose.

Some families have a tradition of being large eaters and some undemonstrative mothers can only show their affection by offering food to family and friends. It certainly seems likely that for mature adults a satisfactory sexual relationship is their most gratifying experience, but that for the infant, happiness lies in being fed and feeling satiated. It is therefore not surprising that many people will react to loss or bereavement by regressing, and attempting to fill the vacuum with food or drink; sadly they may choose the wrong bottle. One obese lady volunteered that the only time she had lost weight was while she was having an affair.

Social and cultural factors are important. There is great emphasis on the desirability of being slim, constantly emphasised in advertising, in magazines, in the fashion industry and among health faddists, despite the fact that in situations of real hardship, as in starvation or exposure to extreme cold, the obese fare better. The problems of the overweight are compounded by feelings of guilt and failure and many actively loathe their bodies.

Very occasionally the complaint of being overweight may be a "red herring", a screen for another problem. One very talented young lady complained of obesity yet was absolutely normal in appearance. She insisted that people would laugh at her fatness if she went out. I suggested that perhaps it was the thought of going out that was frightening and she said, "Yes, I might get lost". She had no memory of being lost at any time but this sounded so like a reactive agoraphobia that I sent her off to cross-examine her elderly mother. She returned to tell me that she had been lost in a supermarket at the age of two, and had spent many hours in a police station before being traced by her devastated parents. I suspect that, in their distress, they had blamed her for wandering off on her own. I have followed this lady's subsequent career with interest and it is reported from all corners of the globe!

Anorexia nervosa has a long history and was described in nuns in the thirteenth century and earlier, as a way of achieving the appearance of virginity. It is said that St Catherine, the patron saint of Sienna, while being conducted to the supper table remarked, "the prisoner is now going to the execution". Anorexia nervosa and bulimia tend to be treated by the psychiatric services so my experience is limited.

I have only records of 25 such patients, all female, with ages ranging from 14 to 36 (average 21) years and the average duration of treatment was sixteen months, though I am probably fortunate that even in this small group there were no deaths. Most more experienced workers report males with anorexia as representing around ten per cent of patients. I have seen only two males who were referred as anorexics, but both had serious organic brain disease.

As medical patients anorexics are notoriously difficult to manage especially as they are so skilled in hiding food and in concealing their vomiting or purging. Many have been in other hospitals where they had been force-fed, albeit fairly kindly. One such patient, on admission, would only speak through clenched teeth! Our routine tended to be to give time for a lot of talking but never to mention food or eating and this studied indifference often served to defuse the problem. Parental sabotage of our efforts was not uncommon as with one patient who had gained around 8 kilos in weight and whose mother said, "You are letting yourself go, you are getting fat!"

Some anorexics seem to begin as mildly overweight teenagers and are genuinely worried about their fatness. They start to slim but become involved in a vicious circle of eating avoidance. Such patients may respond well to behavioural or cognitive therapy. Several of the anorexics I have seen were "only-children" or the youngest in the family, and it has seemed likely that the parents' marriage was unhappy and that the youngster's illness was, in part at least, a stratagem to keep the marriage intact.

It has been noted that anorexia often begins around puberty and that starvation reverses secondary sexual characteristics including menstruation. Certainly I have found that eighty per cent of the patients I have seen have seemed to be singularly compliant as children. The mother frequently says, "She was such an easy child and always did as she was told".

This studied evasion of decision making may well be important since the first individual decision they encounter is whether or not to go out with some young man. The arrest or reversal of secondary sexual traits may be a solution to this dilemma.

Twenty per cent of the anorexics in my group had a background of parents in the catering trade as hotel managers, chefs, etc. To avoid eating may be a successful manoeuvre to influence parental behaviour. It has always been noted that anorexics tend to be interested in cooking for other people but do not themselves eat and this was apparent in sixty-four per cent of my cohort. It seems likely that this characteristic stems from their interest in, and need for food, which they must somehow control. Perhaps the nearest the anorexic can get to the longed-for food, without actually eating it and getting fat, is to cook it and watch others enjoying it. I stumbled on another possible explanation of this behaviour while talking with one patient. She had been buying food in the hospital canteen and offering it to the other patients in the ward. She volunteered the information that, in her childhood her mother had never joined the family at meal time but always went off to the kitchen to prepare the next course or whatever. So perhaps anorexics identify with a mother who feeds everyone but does not herself eat. I began to make a special note of this phenomenon after this episode and in the next seven anorexic patients I encountered, five reported that their mothers had not eaten with the family.

It is, of course, well recognised that recovered anorexics tend to follow careers in catering and I was surprised to find that pharmacy was also a popular career choice and perhaps is regarded as an occupation related to catering.

11. Arthritis

Nay, her foot speaks, her wanton spirits look out
At every joint and motive of her body.

William Shakespeare

The general public and the medical profession are becoming increasingly aware of the importance of diseases of the joints, both as a source of suffering and also as a cost to society in terms of lost earning capacity and an increased financial load on the supporting services. This seems underlined by the rise of rheumatology as a sub-specialty of general medicine.

The osteo-arthritic diseases are mainly related to fair wear and tear and generally affect people in the second half of their life span, although they may begin earlier if their joints have been subjected to unusual physical stresses. The inflammatory and auto-immune disorders are mostly seen in the active and progressive earlier half of life, though some may start relatively late in life, perhaps because some people age more slowly than others, but also because of the associated emotional precipitants.

Antibiotics have almost eliminated the cardiac and joint disorders associated with streptococcal infections and acute rheumatism, although we still occasionally see cases of sub-acute rheumatism in the elderly which are almost identical in appearance with true rheumatoid arthritis. Gout is relatively rare in Scotland but is a diagnostic triumph since the response to correct medication is so gratifying.

In considering the emotional factors in arthritic disease it is most helpful to look at the auto-immune disorders such as true rheumatoid arthritis, ankylosing spondylitis, systemic lupus erythematosus and other collagen disorders, and perhaps we should include psoriatic arthropathy. The arthritic complications of ulcerative colitis and Crohn's disease have many emotional factors in common with the arthropathies considered here.

There appears to be strong evidence that many patients have a life situation of unresolved mourning and a further "bereavement" such as a death, retirement or redundancy causes depression of immunity and allows auto-immune disease to gain a foothold. Some years ago a colleague accosted me in a newsagent's shop and said, "I wish you would see my brother. He has been made redundant and his G P is treating him for a wrench!". The unfortunate man was in fact developing systemic lupus. In addition to this unresolved mourning it seems probable that at the onset of the arthritis there may be powerful feelings of having been defeated by circumstances beyond control.

My records show a group of twenty-four patients of whom seventeen had psychotherapy of an average duration of twenty-seven months. The age range was nineteen to sixty-six (average 38.5) years.

The first patient with whom I attempted a psychosomatic approach was a young man in his twenties with rheumatoid arthritis who was referred because he was unable to take any of the standard medication for arthritis. All the prescribed drugs caused dyspepsia and he was known to have a duodenal ulcer. (Again this demonstrates the frailty of my generalisation regarding patients who internalise or externalise their symptoms, but so be it). The referring colleague knew I was interested in the problems of peptic ulcers and we agreed to admit the young man.

I embarked on psychotherapy directed towards his ulcer problem which was familiar territory for me at that time. He was the eldest of his family and had two younger sisters. The mother was healthy but his father had been a housebound invalid suffering from severe rheumatic heart disease. Identification with rheumatic disease seemed a possible facet of the arthritis. The father had died leaving the patient as the substitute husband and potential breadwinner at the age of fourteen. He trained as an electrician and spent some years working by day for one firm, and also worked as a maintenance electrician most evenings and often all night.

This effort to provide for his mother and sisters resulted in massive bleeding from his ulcer requiring hospital treatment. He felt defeated by this illness and a total failure in his son/husband role and at this stage he began to develop joint pains. He described one occasion from his childhood in which he had completed the construction of a model aircraft and took it to his father's bedroom for approval. The father was, perhaps understandably, envious of his son's fitness and dexterity. He chose not to approve, but to point out various minor defects of alignment and so on. The youngster returned to his own room and smashed the model into tiny fragments feeling that he would never be able to do anything well or to gain his father's approval. He felt this episode had upset his relationship with his father and had certainly interfered with the mourning process when the father died. So in this case both mourning difficulties and feelings o. defeat were fairly obvious. The effect of our discussions wa: that he could soon tolerate massive doses of salicylate medication without discomfort and his joints improved rapidly. After a month in hospital he was able to jog round the hospital grounds and proceeded to make a good recovery.

Encouraged by this experience I attempted to treat a second patient who was referred by a surgical colleague. She was in her mid-thirties and had a short history of small joint pains with a high sedimentation rate but negative serological tests for arthritis. She was highly intelligent and articulate, and despite having left school at the age of fourteen had a most unusual dexterity with words. She was the elder of two girls in the family and the parents were both strict and undemonstrative so that the upbringing had been somewhat rigid and austere. The story unfolded that she had been engaged to be married in her early twenties and had become pregnant. The fiancé talked her into a rather clumsy attempted abortion and she actually miscarried while standing in a cinema queue with the young man. Shortly thereafter he broke off the engagement and disappeared. She had the double "bereavement" of both fiance and child and intense guilt feelings, increased by her rigid family, so it is perhaps not surprising that her joints also became rigid!

We spent several sessions discussing this sad story and she then presented me with a dream which must score highly in my experience of beautiful dreams. She dreamt that she had walked into a huge cathedral which was dark and forbidding. She walked forward to the altar and was upset to see a tiny coffin lying upon it. Behind the altar stood a clergyman in full official finery who quoted chapter and verse from the Bible of her sins. She knelt in tears before the altar and pleaded that it was not all her fault. Eventually she raised her head to find that sunshine was streaming in the windows and the athedral was brightly lit. The clergyman had disappeared and in his place was a cross with the crucified Christ.

Following this dream her sedimentation rate fell rapidly to normal and her joint pains disappeared. She moved to the South of England and for many years held important posts where her creative writing talents were utilised. She eventually returned to Scotland to help and support her ageing parents. Most unfortunately her father died in rather difficult circumstances and at almost the same time she became redundant. Quite rapidly she developed severe mixed collagen disease with positive serology and is severely handicapped. So at best our work together had perhaps only postponed the development of her disease.

Many patients with rheumatoid arthritis are difficult subjects for psychotherapy as they often seem unconsciously to be undergoing a self-punishment process and have a somewhat martyred attitude to their illness. They complain surprisingly little about their discomfort and this often has a spin off effect on their children. I have seen patients with other illnesses who are reluctant to ask for medical help or who seem singularly uncomplaining in the presence of severe pain. I frequently found that they had a parent who suffered from rheumatoid arthritis. "Mother never complained!"

It is encouraging to encounter patients with arthritis who are determinedly aggressive and undefeated by the illness and they make good subjects for psychotherapy.

It is obvious, of course, that arthritic patients should have the benefit of any medical or surgical treatment which proved helpful. One lady was seen because she appeared to be unable to tolerate any of the standard remedies for early, but sero-positive rheumatoid arthritis. She did not have a peptic ulcer but had always shown intolerance to drugs and to alcohol. Psychotherapy had been advised as a kind of last, if slender, hope. The initial interview was promising as she had intelligence, insight and humour.

Her story was that soon after her son was born she and her husband went off to a remote part of the North of Scotland to visit his parents and to introduce the new arrival to the grandparents. Her husband, who had a history of asthma, developed severe status asthmaticus in the home environment. There was no telephone and as my patient was the only driver, she set off to get medical help. On her return she was shattered to find that her husband had died. When I saw the patient her son was eight and had recently developed eczema and asthma and this was probably a factor in precipitating her arthritis. Her parents shared his care and she spoke of fears that the extra load would kill her mother, almost certainly as an early childhood threat in her own life. In the course of therapy she worked through the relationship with her parents and the process of letting go of her late husband. She was able to see in her dreams that she could make new relationships and has subsequently re-married. After a year of psychotherapy and without any specific medication the patient's symptoms improved and to my astonishment her serological tests became negative. A ten year follow-up has shown no return of joint symptoms.

In some instances one can almost see an element of body language symbolism in arthritic patients. One patient had a husband who suffered a coronary heart attack and was almost totally defeated by his illness. He was very apprehensive and would scarcely lift the morning paper in case he strained his heart. After some months of doing all the lifting and carrying, from trays to suitcases, his wife developed classical sero-positive rheumatoid arthritis but almost only affecting her upper limbs.

12. Internalised disorders

Now the will, I fear, is less master of the mind than
of the body. A man may resolve never to move
from his chair, but he cannot never to be angry.

Peter Mere Latham

As suggested in Chapter Two, there seems to be a group of
people who internalise their stresses and react by producing
spasm of smooth circular muscle. As we have no voluntary
control over our autonomic nervous system, which operates
on our internal organs, these internal disorders are often
treated by drugs designed to counteract the output of the
sympathetic or parasympathetic pathways, and with some
success. It is tempting to believe that the autonomic nervous
system is strongly affected by our feelings and challenging to
wonder whether a psychotherapeutic approach might modify
our reactions and emotions and so assist in improving the
condition. We must remember that there are also other
factors such as familial or truly genetic components or

genuine allergies in many of these disorders and accept that the emotional contribution is only part of the picture. Equally I would emphasise that to ignore this component may prolong suffering.

We refer to patients with raised blood pressure as suffering from hypertension and the state of their constricted spastic arterioles may well be the result of a long standing state of raised emotional tension. Some researchers have even postulated that from their early days these patients were constantly forbidden to indulge in the simple mischief-making of childhood and developed a state of continued frustration and thwarted rebellion. Certainly, by adult life, a true sustained hypertension seems to be a fixed lesion which has passed the point of no return and which requires drug treatment to avoid disaster. I have tried, totally without success, to modify true hypertension and I doubt whether psychological modification is either possible or justified. That being said, it is important to be aware of people with labile blood pressure who may be wrongly diagnosed and treated as sustained hypertension.

Many patients are referred to consultant physicians for assessment of their raised blood pressure yet show no evidence of the stigmata of hypertension, such as retinal changes, cardiac enlargement, cardiograph abnormalities or renal damage. These require very sophisticated appraisal and I can offer only one suggestion. I noticed that these patients were reluctant to be admitted to hospital for assessment and it occurred to me that they disliked the whole medical setup. I began to wonder if their blood pressure only rose at the sight of a stethoscope. It soon became obvious that most of them had been in hospital before the age of five and that in many instances this had been an infectious diseases hospital where no visitors were allowed. Clearly the child who is banished to hospital and denied visits from parents is likely to equate illness with punishment and nurses as threatening authority figures. A tape is recorded which plays back in adult life, quite out of context, but which can readily be switched off once the original reason for this reaction is brought to consciousness.

One illustrative case history should suffice. An obstetrician wrote, "Could you please see this twenty-three year old girl as an urgent case. She is in her first pregnancy and I make her blood pressure 230/180". My examination showed a similar blood pressure reading with a fast heart rate and increased knee jerks, but her ophthalmic appearances were of pristine normality. So I pulled up a chair and we talked.

"Do you remember being in hospital as a small child?"
"Oh yes; I was only three but could never forget it".
"And what was your illness".
"I had meningitis and I was the only one in the ward who did not die".

After a few minutes of discussion I repeated the blood pressure reading - 120/80 and so it remained throughout her pregnancy.

I have sometimes suggested to these patients that, like Brer Rabbit, we all have a "laughing place" where we remember being totally relaxed and happy. If they are about to have a blood pressure recording for insurance purposes or for fitness for flying, they should go to their "laughing place" and all will be well!

With the possible exception of asthmatics most of the patients in this group who internalise under stress are "Type A" personalities - the virtuous obsessionals who use incessant activity as justification and as a defence against their imagined emotional inadequacy. Their early life was often characterised by undemonstrative parents who emphasised punctuality, cleanliness and industry. "Anyone who is doing nothing is doing something wrong." School reports were scrutinised in detail and good results were insufficiently approved and rewarded. One patient recalled telling his mother he had a mark of 98% in his German examination and the reply was, "What did you do with the other two marks?"

Patients who present with internalised disorders may have had added responsibilities thrust on them at too early an age as happens to older daughters in large families and to older sons if their father dies. They seem to have missed out on the pleasures of leisure and play and part of the therapy is to help them to relax without feeling guilty and to relearn the art of laughter.

These patients often have difficulty in expressing anger and resentment and tend to turn their anger back on themselves. They have difficulty in blowing off steam as a safety valve and tend to bottle up anger till the boiler blows up. Occasionally this produces an outburst of physical or verbal violence but often is internalised and the ulcer bleeds or perforates or they have a heart attack or a cerebral vascular catastrophe.

13. Migraine

Here is a grotto, shelter'd close from air,
And screen'd in shades from day's detested glare,
She sighs forever on her pensive bed,
Pain at her side, and Megrim at her head.

Alexander Pope

Migraine is a relatively common condition and many sufferers appear to have attacks which are induced by eating tyramine-containing foods. These are fairly easy to spot if they can eat black chocolate (or drink chianti) without suffering later. They respond well to suitable medication. Some cases are triggered by glare or by flashing lights in a fashion similar to that seen in photopic epilepsy. A number of migraine sufferers have a background of mild depression and there is a correlation between migraine and premenstrual tension, probably on account of the fluid retention encountered at that stage of the cycle. Migraine tends to start in the mid-teens though there is often a previous history of bilious attacks or of cyclical vomiting. A family history is common and almost all suffer more in emotionally stressful situations.

Migraine differs from most of the other psychosomatic disorders in that there may be quite a long gap between the precipitating emotional event and the onset of headache. Dyspepsia and bronchospasm are often closely related in time to some stressful situation, but the gap in migraine may be up to forty-eight hours. This probably explains why migraine is present on waking or begins in apparently relaxed spells with no obvious stress being detectable.

It is certainly profitable to correct any minor physical disability such as anaemia, refractive error or ocular muscle imbalance. It is vitally important to review the diagnosis and to avoid the pitfall of overlooking serious intracranial mischief such as aneurysm of the Circle of Willis or a cerebral tumour. As always one should review the transference situation before embarking on a physical re-examination. Amusing episodes can occur, as in the case of one delightful patient whose migraine was so severe that I carried out an ophthalmoscopic examination at every consultation to exclude raised intracranial pressure. It gradually transpired that that she was resentful of her husband, whose jealousy almost amounted to paranoia. I suggested that her husband might be upset at her coming to see a physician and she said, "After the last visit he asked what I was doing with that man for a whole hour?" "And what did you say to that?" I asked and she replied "I told him you looked into my eyes!"

Migraine accounts for seventy-eight patients in my series, of whom sixty-one had psychotherapy for an average of eighteen months. The age range was fifteen to fifty-four (average 33) years. My clinical impression was that the patients tend to be of high intelligence and to be obsessional. They often developed an attack when they felt resentful but unable to deal with the provocative situation. A rough analysis of my group tends to confirm this impression as 88% had high intelligence, 68% were obsessional and 82% showed a cause associated with resentment.

The feeling of resentment and frustration may be fairly obvious, as in one patient in her thirties, who had a three months history of migraine. She had been in the United States in a post which was interesting and challenging but had to return to Scotland to look after her sick and elderly parents. At her first visit she stated that she felt resentful that the demands of her parents had upset her successful career and interrupted her friendships abroad, but was also aware that, as the only child, she had little option. The opportunity to ventilate and to share this emotional load seemed to improve her migraine.

Another patient, aged forty, presented with a history of migraine since the age of eighteen but the story was unusual in that she claimed the headache was often triggered by doing housework. She had a supportive husband and two splendid sons and seemed to be coping well with her life situation. The underlying emotional mechanism was quite straightforward. Her mother had died when she was aged fifteen and as the only daughter she took over the mother's role and looked after her father and elder brother. She devoted herself to tasks of homework, shopping, cooking and laundry and no doubt missed out on many opportunities for leisure and recreation as a result.

When she was eighteen her father remarried. She felt rejected by her father in her attempt to act as a substitute for his deceased wife and felt resentful that her efforts as a housekeeper must have been considered unsatisfactory. Not surprisingly she had at least unconscious doubts about her role as a wife in her own home and it is easy to understand why her migraine was precipitated by housework. She had a quick and creative mind and her therapy proceeded apace. The first dream offered was that a large hole had been dug in the garden to make a swimming pool. It had filled with water and a workman had fallen in, so she dived in to rescue him.

This suggested that she was able to explore the depth of her own psyche without feeling endangered. Thereafter came a series of dreams associated with descent from heights, by sledging with her children or driving her car down steep hills but always well under control, perhaps as she came down from her thinking to her feeling life. Several dreams included dogs, which are usually feminine in dreams and certainly she was showing more confidence in her feminine role. The migraine rapidly changed to minor headaches. Then there came a dream in which she fired a rifle at her father's head but only made a hole in his hat. This was apparently enough to let the devils out as there were no more headaches. Her final dream was that the swimming pool was now complete so I took the hint and we parted company.

Occasionally the diagnosis is in doubt and a spell of discussion and observation may be of value. One man of forty-five gave a history of headaches from later school days but of increasing severity in the last ten years. His maternal grandmother had suffered from migraine and his father had frequent headaches. In early childhood he had experienced a severe head injury and his mother constantly reminded him of how near he had been to death's door. To add to the confusion the headaches were much worse at the weekends so it seemed likely that there was some domestic stress but the only information offered was that his son was adopted. Both the patient's parents had been school teachers and he identified strongly with them and wished to be a teacher. His father discouraged this as "there was no money in it." So surprise, surprise, he became a banker!

Indeed the only spell in which he was completely free of headaches was while he was in the services where he was employed in teaching duties. He was rather resistant to any idea of an emotional factor on his headaches, but I noted that had a marked disparity in the refraction of his two eyes and had a quite obvious ocular muscle imbalance. A review of his refraction and a course of orthoptic treatment improved his headache. I feel it would be uncharitable to imply that this gave him a respectable excuse to get better!

Premenstrual migraine is common and it is possible that there is an element of water retention acting as a trigger factor. Many such patients had parents who never discussed the problems and functions of menstruation and often called it "the curse". These sufferers can readily be helped by psychotherapeutic discussion.

Again each patient is unique and must be so regarded. I recall many years ago being asked to see a woman in her late forties who had incapacitating migraine. She had been extensively investigated in London and had had many forms of treatment including a spell of Freudian analysis. Her advisers had decided that the migraine resulted from the undoubted trauma of her husband being killed in the army during the second world war. There was no doubt that the condition was worse from this time but she did have migraine from her late teens. She claimed that she never recalled her dreams so the conversation proceeded as follows.

"Do you draw or paint or even doodle when speaking on the telephone?"
"Oh yes, I doodle and I always draw flags."
"And for whom had you to carry the banner?"
"My goodness, that is when my migraine started."

The story was one which I found familiar She had been brought up in the West Highlands and as the cleverest of the family was singled out for a university career, while her brothers and sisters were sent off to work and earn money for her education. She failed her examinations and felt she had let the family down and the headaches started. She improved considerably over the next two years but continued to have occasional migraine.

14. Coronary heart disease

His flaw'd heart,
Alack! Too weak the conflict to support;
'Twixt two extremes of passion, joy and grief,
Burst smilingly.

William Shakespeare

Anyone intrepid enough to discuss the role of the emotions
in coronary disease exposes himself to stresses that are
asserted by some to be lethal.

H B Sprague

Under this heading it is relevant to discuss ischaemic heart
disease as a cause of angina pectoris, as well as of true
coronary occlusion. Many of the features of personality and
behaviour of these patients also characterise patients with the
"heart-ache" syndrome who may show no evidence of heart
disease initially, but who are nevertheless likely to develop
demonstrable changes or actual disease if they are dismissed
as cardiac neurosis, or are reassured without adequate
emotional investigation.

Angina pectoris, as a description of symptoms has probably

been recognised for hundreds of years, while in the 18th and 19th centuries morbid anatomists described the postmortem appearances of coronary artery disease and of "myomalacia cordis". The first clinical diagnosis of coronary thrombosis made during the patient's life is attributed to Hammer (27) in Vienna in 1876. In British medical literature the earliest paper on **The Syndrome of Coronary Thrombosis** was by J W McNee (28) in 1925. Ischaemic heart disease has become increasingly common throughout the present century and is a frequent cause of death in western countries. According to the Registrar General, in 1931, 832 deaths in Scotland were certified as due to ischaemic heart disease. This had risen to 10,762 by 1960 and to 18,758 by 1985. Indeed Scotland leads the world in its incidence of coronary heart disease.

The condition is much commoner in males and it is interesting that female hormones appear to provide protection until the menopause or the surgeon intervenes. It is perhaps less well known that during pregnancy the cholesterol and lipid pattern changes to resemble that of the male (Oliver & Boyd (29)) and that ischaemic disorders and actual myocardial infarctions occasionally occur during pregnancy.

The medical profession has a higher incidence of coronary disease than occurs in other occupations and this may well be part of the reason why the emotional component tends to be so strenuously denied while great emphasis is placed on factors such as diet, exercise and smoking. All these are indubitably important but it is intriguing to read comments such as those of Arnott (30) on the effects of stress and strain - "So far as I can see this hypothesis has no scientifically creditable basis whatsoever; in fact most of the evidence adduced in its support is dubious and much of it is absurd".

Fortunately more enlightened investigators have clarified our knowledge of the personality features of this type of patient such as the description of the "Type A" personality by Friedman and his colleagues (14). They also demonstrated that the blood levels of cholesterol and other lipids varied with stress of either an occupational or domestic variety (31).

My earlier scepticism regarding the emotional component in coronary disease was abruptly altered in 1956 when I was carrying out a home visit. As I recorded the cardiogram which showed a small recent anterior infarction the patient volunteered the information that his pain had started shortly after his homosexual partner had come to visit him and had taken his young sister out for the evening!

Over the years I have, I hope, widened my assessment of these patients. They certainly conform to the "Type A" personality with marked features of drive, ambition and almost obsessional conscientiousness. The early environment tended to be strict and often the father died young so that they identify with "the good father" and strive to be similar. As a result these people are usually kind and caring towards their dependents and colleagues. They are reluctant to ask for medical help especially if their partner is on holiday and might be inconvenienced. They strive to climb the ladder of success but will give a helping hand to others on the way. They lack the streak of ruthlessness which is often present in peptic ulcer patients who are quite capable of kicking their colleagues off the ladder as they pass by.

Coronary patients or potential patients tend to be "do-gooders", in the best sense, so have a strong sense of vocation and choose occupations such as medicine, the church or social work to suit this need. In addition to their main occupation, many have a second "job" in Trade Union activity or in church, musical or youth organisations. These characteristics are quite independent of social class. One of my house physicians teased me that he had admitted a man with a "coronary" who did not fit my theory as he worked for the local authority keeping a leisurely eye on the state of rural roadways. So I asked the patient what else he did and he replied, "Oh, I am the village chimney sweep and I sweep two chimneys most mornings before I start work".

One evening some years ago I took a group of my medical students to see a seventy-five year old man who had been admitted with a myocardial infarction. We discussed his life style and he told us how he had recently retired for the third time. I shook my head and said to the students, "Some people have a need to drive racing cars" and the patient interjected, "Oh, I do that too, doctor".

Perhaps the most important feature of the group and a key diagnostic marker is that these patients find it almost impossible to say "No" to requests or demands. I find this such a predominant characteristic that I use it as a yardstick in attempting to modify the behaviour of angina sufferers or of convalescent myocardial infarction patients. If they can learn to say "No" they are less likely to have progressive angina or a further heart attack.

Superimposed upon this personality background there comes a final precipitant, a roll of drums, which results in the crisis. This is often a feeling of guilt or inadequacy; these patients feel perhaps that they have failed someone who needed their help. They feel angry with themselves and seem to turn the anger inwards in a kind of sophisticated suicide attempt. This type of reaction was exemplified by a patient in his early forties who had a severe myocardial infarction. He occupied a senior position in the electric power industry and was on call for emergencies. In his spare time he tutored sixth formers in physics and mathematics. His chest pain developed while he was talking on the telephone to one of his pupils who had just failed his "A level" mathematics.

A number of patients almost literally break their hearts. One man developed his myocardial infarction when his sixteen year old daughter announced that she was pregnant. Another very sad example was a man who was admitted with his third "coronary" at the early age of thirty-five years. It transpired hat he had married at the age of twenty-one. His wife continued to work and he usually reached home before her and organised the evening meal before she returned. After a year of happiness the wife developed leukaemia and died. The patient was unable to accept this tragedy and at the age of thirty-five was still coming home from work and laying the supper table for two people. I believe that had he been able to "let go" of his wife and accept the situation, he might well have re-married, had a family, and avoided developing a "broken heart".

The physical management of patients with acute myocardial infarction has altered vastly over the past twenty years. Most patients, especially in the younger age group, are admitted to coronary care units and are subjected to continuous electronic surveillance. Some patients undoubtedly find this reassuring though some subsequently describe the experience as making them feel isolated and depersonalised. I hope that some day both coronary care units and intensive care units will employ a psychodynamically trained counsellor as part of the service they offer, as is done in the more enlightened oncology units. Both the staff and patients are grateful for expert support in these stressful areas of medical care.

In some instances even the decision to admit the patient to hospital involves difficult decisions. I recall seeing a man with a moderately extensive myocardial infarction in his own home. While I was examining him and taking an electrocardiogram I noted that his eyes never left his wife who was moving around the room. I felt he was unusually dependent upon this lady and suggested to the G P that if at all possible we should try to manage the patient at home, though I agreed to admit him if there was any further indication to do so. He arrived in my hospital unit the following day and when I went to see him I noticed that the book lying on his bedside locker was entitled **The Last Journey** and so it proved to be. In all probability the outcome would have been similar had he stayed at home but I still have a guilty feeling that I had failed in my management of this patient.

Many "coronary" patients resent their illness and feel guilty at being off duty though they tend to hide their feelings. They respond well to a policy of providing full information and of being encouraged to share responsibility for their recovery. An autocratic approach is likely to end in disaster.

I thought originally that it might be unwise to become involved in the psyche of these patients during their acute illness. However a series of patients appeared to have persistent pain, fast heart rates and intractable insomnia and it seemed that there was little to lose by encouraging them to talk. To my surprise they almost invariably had significant emotional and social problems, such as invalid wives, business crises and so on and allowing them to ventilate their misgivings almost always improved their physical state and probably helped in their eventual recovery. So my first foray into the problems of these patients was with the severely ill and this encouraged me to try to have at least one long discussion with all these patients before they left hospital. I now wish I had kept records of these interviews. With encouragement the convalescents often see their priorities more clearly and can rearrange their life style to avoid further illness. They have an opportunity to ask specific questions and one gradually learns some of the emotional pitfalls.

For example, many men would ask when they could resume sexual relationships and this question had to be clarified rather than answered. Most found that their sex life was a vital and important part of their existence but quite a number found it difficult or threatening and were, in fact, asking either for permission to desist from such activity or for help in overcoming their feelings of inadequacy, if not actual impotence.

Many patients are able to accept their illness and some limitation of their activity in a philosophical manner, without demonstrating either fear for the future or undue recklessness. Some indeed have later said that their heart attack had been of benefit in allowing them to enjoy life more fully and realistically.

Exceptions occur at both ends of the scale. Some patients deny their illness and question the diagnosis. This "defiant" group return early to work and activity. One colleague insisted on going to the local swimming baths daily and demonstrating his fitness to his patients by prolonged spells of underwater swimming. At the other end of the scale are the "defeated" who become regressed and dependent and live in terror of a further episode. Both these groups appear to fare badly in terms of survival.

As the District General Hospital in which I worked had a fairly closed community catchment area we attempted a ten year retrospective assessment of our myocardial infarction patients. 660 patients had been admitted, some on more than one occasion, with a total of 726 unequivocal infarctions and of these 273 (36%) died in hospital. A small group of 43, all severely ill, had a spell of psychotherapeutic support of whom 2 (4.6%) died in hospital. We attempted to trace the survivors after a five year gap to see how many had further episodes or had died, and traced 344 patients. As the psychotherapy group were all under sixty-five years of age they were compared with the survivors in the same age group. While accepting that the number of patients having psychotherapy was small it is interesting that 78% were alive and well on follow up as compared with 55% of the psychotherapeutically untreated group.

I then began to keep more detailed records of patients with ischaemic heart disease and these are noted in Appendix TABLE B. My records show 33 patients with ischaemic heart disease who were studied in a psychodynamic fashion. The age range was 26-65 (average 39.5) years and 26 were males. 21 patients had psychotherapy with an average duration of 20 months. 91% of this group were classified as obsessional and 85% had two "jobs". Only 18% were smokers, while only 6% asserted that they could say "No" to demands.

A few illustrative case histories may help to show the variety of the life situations encountered though the main features are often similar. A fifty-two year old man was admitted with an extensive myocardial infarction. He came from outside the area and had been visiting a factory locally to assess fire damage for his employers, an insurance company. He had been brought up in a Lanarkshire mining village as the youngest of a large family. His father had been injured in a mining accident and had an alcohol problem. While he was still in primary school his eldest brother had banished the alcoholic parent from the household.

A couple of years later the patient was playing football for his school team in the next village and the rejected father came to watch the match. Afterwards his father took him to the local shops and bought him a splendid gift of a new pair of football boots. On returning home the elder brother asked about the new boots and on hearing of the donor, made the lad watch while he burned the new boots on the kitchen fire. And so my patient had become a fire insurance assessor!

At this time the elder brother also told the boy that he was in fact the son of his eldest sister. So father had to be re-orientated as grandfather, and in addition he felt overwhelmingly rejected by his real mother. So there must have been a precipitant of the present illness. It transpired that the patient had been at a business celebration dinner the previous evening and had returned home slightly tipsy. His own son had threatened that if his father ever got drunk again he would be banished from his home. I have no doubt that this further rejection and the strong identification with his father (grandfather) was an important factor in his subsequent heart attack. We had many discussions over the next few months and he returned to work in good health.

The next example was really a challenge from a colleague who asked me to see an orchestral player who had partially recovered from a massive infarction. My colleague was suggesting that this patient would never be able to cope again with a French horn. The patient certainly seemed rather defeated. He had lost his own father when aged ten and had helped to support his widowed mother throughout his teens. Before the present illness he had a full-time orchestral post and also taught pupils in every spare moment. As his own father had never been around he did not consider his presence necessary in the family circle, but did feel it was important to make money to help his only daughter if anything should happen to him.

He had recently employed an acquaintance of his own age to decorate his house. He returned from a rehearsal one day to find a note from his daughter saying that she had eloped with the painter. It seems likely that she had never had a father figure around the house and had probably some unconscious confusion over the roles. The patient set off to the home of the decorator which meant climbing three flights of tenement stairs. A neighbour then told him that the couple had left for the registry office to be married. As he descended the stairs he developed severe chest pain. The psychotherapy sessions were often stormy but in the end he relinquished all his teaching commitments and was able to return to successful orchestral playing.

A paradoxical tale may also be helpful. This patient was admitted with a very extensive myocardial infarction and was much more aggressive and resentful of hospital treatment than is usual even in this somewhat difficult group of patients. He strenuously denied that he was ill and insisted he be allowed home. He was sixty years of age and was a probation officer who was trained in psychological casework. His attitude was rather difficult to understand until the apparent paradox became evident. It appeared that on the eve of his own marriage many years previously, his father had collapsed and died of a coronary thrombosis. His own illness had occurred on the eve of his son's wedding and he therefore felt that this was just a reactivation of his own upset of earlier years and could not possibly be the real thing.

It is likely that any strong emotion may precipitate an attack and this may even be a pleasant emotion. In our male ward there worked a fair-haired probationer nurse who looked rather non-descript in her uniform. One evening the senior registrar of the unit was coming into the hospital when he met this nurse on her way out to a dance. In her evening dress she looked so stunning that he immediately propelled her into a lift and up into the male ward where she worked. A seventy year old man sat up in bed, gave a wolf whistle and fell back dead of a myocardial infarction. One of my colleagues suggested that this was the only "double blonde trial" in my series!

Patients with angina may also benefit from a psychological assessment of the symptoms. A very shrewd and experienced family doctor asked me to see a patient aged fifty suffering from angina of effort. As he and I climbed several flights of stairs to her home he remarked that the real puzzle was that she climbed these stairs without discomfort yet had pain walking on level ground. Our examination and E C G revealed definite, if minor, ischaemia only. So I asked more about her pain and found that she only had it while walking to visit her elderly mother in an old people's home. It finally emerged that her husband had threatened to divorce her, unless her mother left their home and was admitted to alternative care, a decision which left her with much unresolved guilt.

Another guilt-ridden example was of a man whose routine was to have a Sunday evening walk with his wife and family. If church bells were heard he developed severe chest pain and had to return home. His parents had been enthusiastic Salvation Army officials and church three times every Sunday had been an unbreakable rule!

A fifty year old engineer was referred as he had persistent angina even at rest in bed one year after having a small inferior myocardial infarction. Some attacks were truly exertional but he asked why he also developed pain as he put the key into his front door, and also experienced his worst attacks while at rest in bed, adding as an afterthought, "When I have that nightmare". At the very least it seemed that entering his home caused some kind of apprehension and I ignored any sexual connotation of keys and keyholes. But the nightmare was recurrent and in it he was trying to open a window and could never manage to do so. Since windows are apertures which do not reach down to the floor, I could now only suggest that there might be some emotional upset at home leading to a state of sexual frustration. The patient was surprised but also relieved at this remark and told me he had not slept with his spouse for sixteen years. Thereafter the nightmare and nocturnal angina ceased but he remained to some extent disabled.

I mentioned above the occasional cases of coronary disease in pregnancy. In the 1950s and 1960s cardiograph changes which would have been accepted as definite myocardial infarctions were blandly described as cases of cardiomyopathy of pregnancy. In 1952 Erskine (32) had reported a case in which coronary thrombosis was confirmed by a postmortem examination. My interest was aroused by the reports from Edinburgh of the lipid changes in pregnancy. I was able to observe and investigate twelve such cases, one being confirmed as a myocardial infarction at autopsy. My search for an emotional component was not very rewarding and fairly predictable. Most patients were relatively "elderly" (36 years plus) and half of them were highly multiparous, being in their sixth to thirteenth pregnancy, and not surprisingly were often anxious or resentful. The youngest patient was only nineteen and had developed an inferior myocardial infarction at 24 weeks gestation. She was unmarried at the time of conception and had been subjected to much pressure to accept a termination. Eventually the couple married and the pregnancy and a subsequent one were successful.

15. Asthma

*Asthmatics should be on guard
against their own anger.*

Hippocrates

Asthma is a distressing condition for both the sufferer and the
observer and carries significant threats for an untimely
demise. In clinical practice it is useful to assess whether the
patient has intermittent bouts of asthma or whether he or she
is in an almost constant state of bronchospasm. The
intermittent wheezers, even though their attacks may be
severe, appear to fare better than the chronic constant
wheezers who tend to develop severe right heart strain at an
early stage. Some, before the age of thirty, show cardiograph
changes normally associated with elderly patients with long
standing chronic bronchitis, emphysema, or obstructive
airways disease

I try to assess the contribution to the illness of three components, infection, allergy and emotional stress and to decide which is the main factor. Upper respiratory infection will often trigger an attack of asthma and this is normally fairly obvious, but it is important to remember the possibility of less common infections such as aspergillosis.

The contribution of an allergic response is of most importance in truly atopic subjects who may show other manifestations like eczema or hay fever and who have high levels of serum IgE on laboratory testing. A search for specific allergens by a careful history, by skin tests or other methods may be rewarding. The patient may be able to avoid exposure to the offending substance and occasionally may be desensitised. Certain types of medication may be more effective in patients with a large allergic component in their disorder. Skin sensitivity tests in my experience, only rarely demonstrate one specific agent; most asthmatics seem to react to many or all of the test stimuli.

The actual process of testing has its own value as it takes time and if the patient can be encouraged to talk during this time, other important, if non-allergic stimuli, may be found. I believe it is very worthwhile to look at the symbolism of the positive results as this may be highly informative. Females who are allergic to eggs are often either childless or have at least twelve children! Many who react to house dust are slightly resentful of their housekeeping role and miss their previous employment. My only patient who was strongly allergic to feathers and with positive skin tests was a Miss Robin. As can be imagined she had been teased inordinately. One patient reacted strongly to the entire range of skin tests. I asked "Why are you allergic to everything?" and she replied, "That is because my husband is a professional crook and every penny I spend has probably been stolen."

One male asthmatic claimed he was allergic to cats yet skin tests were strongly positive for fish, and for fish only. As he was a marine biologist this information was withheld, but when he was persuaded to watch a film about cats he developed severe asthma. So much for foreign protein! The story underlying this result was that he had been brought up as the only child in a single parent family. His somewhat eccentric mother had ten cats and their fish had to be cooked and served before the child was allowed to eat.

Modern high technology medicine has developed many effective ways of treating asthmatics and continues to search for abstruse relationships to climate, season, time of attacks and so on. Little is taught about the emotional components, save to acknowledge their presence and to imply that nothing can be done about them anyway.

So if we attempt to grasp this nettle it becomes obvious that two emotional areas are worth our consideration. Apart from obvious factors such as identification with "chesty" parents it seems common to find that some asthmatics have parents, and especially mothers, who tend to be over anxious, so that the child is "smothered" and not surprisingly, finds difficulty in breathing. Certainly it is natural that once asthma begins the mother will often be frightened and will become over-protective but the child has usually been fighting for an independent existence earlier. One forty-five year old bachelor was admitted in status asthmaticus and after seeing him I was speaking to his seventy year old mother who said, "You see, doctor, he just won't wear warm socks!!"

Another glimpse of this process came from a young lady whom I asked if she had nightmares before her asthmatic attacks began. She replied, "Oh yes, I dream I am in a room which is getting smaller and smaller and darker". She paused and a look of terror came over her face - "but it's not a room, it's a mouth". A classical example of the "devouring mother" of the early analytic literature. Dr H E Pelser of Amsterdam, who is the most astute observer of patients' behaviour of my acquaintance, once advised that when dealing with asthmatics we should never lean forward in our chair as they will almost certainly start to wheeze.

The other important stress factor is that asthma is a disorder of separation. The condition often starts when the child goes to school or after a change to secondary school or college or following a break in a relationship such as a quarrel, a jilting or a bereavement. In the early days many of my asthmatic patients had fathers who had been prisoners of war, and one can image the anxiety and desolation of the wife and mother and this would spill over, like a waterfall, on to the child.

Many years ago a distant relative telephoned me to say that she was having her first bout of asthma for over twenty years. I could only remember her father had been a sea captain who died when his ship was torpedoed in the First World War. I asked about her twenty-one year old son and she said, "He left for Canada by sea yesterday". We talked about separation anxiety and the unconscious fear that her son, too would be drowned and the wheeze subsided totally as we spoke.

I wrote in an earlier chapter of how psychosomatic patients very seldom show secondary gain and in my experience it has only been the asthmatics who have done so. One severe asthmatic had a husband who was a highly qualified Master Mariner but he had to work as a shipyard labourer as his wife became more ill if he went to sea. Another patient was an outstanding teacher who was admitted to hospital and my ward sister in an unguarded moment said, "Dr. Macdonald will cure your asthma". When I went into her room next morning she announced, "I dreamt last night that you came in here and cut off my toe". It appeared that the asthma always occurred in the run up to public examinations for her fifth and sixth year pupils. I suggested that her asthma was unlikely to be cured as she needed it as an excuse to justify any feelings of failure that might arise when the examination results appeared. To my surprise her asthma rapidly settled. One year later her G P telephoned to say the asthma had re-started.

I said, "Give her my kind regards and say that a small operation on her foot might be required!". Within half an hour the G P telephoned me again to say, "What did that message mean? She is back to normal and off to school".

As shown in Appendix TABLE B my own records include 101 asthmatic patients fairly equally divided between the sexes with ages ranging from 11 to 61 (average 33.7). 69 had psychotherapy of an average duration of twenty months. Relatively few showed obsessional traits (19%). In 51% there was a family history of chest disease and in 75% there was a relevant episode of separation or bereavement.

Again I offer a few case histories. A forty year old man had severe asthma and eczema throughout his whole life. He was a very proficient professional mathematician so he tended to be very logical and it took some months to get him to accept the symbolism of his dreams. His mother had died at his birth and he was convinced (perhaps correctly) that his father and older siblings implied that, but for him, the mother would still be alive. His early dreams were of sitting examinations and anxious to do well but of being inadequately prepared. He slowly began to describe his need to repay his mother by being an intellectual and academic success.

Together we worked through his mourning of his mother and his problems with authority figures whom he expected to be critical like his father. He slowly improved over many months and towards the end of his therapy he gave a summary of the proceedings. He said, "When I came to you I had spent years looking back at my life to find the reasons for my illness and its relationship to my mother's death. I was like an unfurnished room and I didn't know how to furnish it. When we talked I began to realise the things that were missing from my life rather than what had happened. I realised how different it would have been if my mother had lived and I think I can now accept myself and the world". I see this statement as a very useful insight into the mechanism of the psychotherapeutic process.

Another patient who had experienced an early bereavement was first seen in her early forties with a twenty-five years history of hay fever but only a three to four years history of asthma. She had been born in South Africa and when she was four her father died of pulmonary tuberculosis, which suggests that there was at least some identification in her chest symptoms. Her mother came back to Great Britain after her husband's death and worked as a housekeeper in various boarding schools, so that the patient had repeated changes of school and surroundings throughout her life. On skin testing she was sensitive to house dust and to animal fur. Her first fairly transient bronchospasm occurred at twenty-nine when her mother died, and the most severe bout of asthma she experienced during our collaboration was when a close friend died. She was an extremely competent occupational therapist in charge of a large department. Her early dreams were almost all about wild animals. I suggested that she might be using these animals as an expression of feelings which she felt were dangerous and uncontrollable and this led to her being able to express much anger and resentment especially directed towards her father who had "deserted" her.

After this session she dreamt she was driving her car when it suddenly changed into a donkey. She could see that she was making a joke at her own expense and I suggested that her animals, and therefore her feelings, were now able to be trained, controlled and guided to perform useful functions. Shortly thereafter she had a bout of 'flu and bronchitis but with no bronchospasm, which is always an encouraging event in asthmatics' progress.

After being perfectly well for some months she went on holiday to Scandinavia and on her return arrived to see me in a somewhat aggressive frame of mind and with good reason.

Whilst sunbathing on a beach during the holiday she had picked up a handful of sand and let it trickle through her fingers. She immediately developed severe bronchospasm which required hospital treatment. Clearly we had left some stone unturned. She tried free association and very soon described how, when aged three or four, her mother used to visit her sick husband in hospital every afternoon. As he had tuberculosis she was not allowed to visit. She spent many lonely and anxious hours in the hospital grounds playing in the children's sandpit and no doubt feeling that she was responsible for her father's illness and would aggravate it if she visited him. She could recall the feeling of sand trickling through her fingers!

Another patient in his early twenties was a student of architecture who painted pictures of his dreams during his treatment. He was married to a beautiful nurse and they had a six month old son. He had had asthma from the age of seven until sixteen and this had recurred six months before I saw him, so it appeared to coincide with the birth of his son. This young man's mother sounded splendid and, not surprisingly, she also had been a nurse so we looked for separation. His father had been in the regular army and he always wheezed if his father telephoned him. At the age of seven he had been sent to boarding school - the first separation. He then discovered that he had been sent to school so that his parents could "separate" and they were subsequently divorced - the second separation seemed to initiate his asthma.

The first painting of a dream which he offered showed a number of soldiers firing guns while in the foreground he was trying to play a guitar. He described how miserable he felt at school where he had to play rugby and war games in the cadets when he would rather have been painting or making music. He was able to "ventilate" his aggression regarding his father and his occupation, and to accept that he himself was a different kind of man. The asthma had cleared when he left school but recurred when his son was born as he could only identify with unsuccessful fathers. He made rapid progress and after a visit from his mother he produced another picture which was a remarkable example of the archetypal dream and could almost have been taken from one of Jung's books. The main object in the picture was an old sailing ship; he knew that ships were always described as feminine, and he felt that this ship was his mother now sailing quietly out of his life. In the foreground were two almost identical modern power boats which he saw as his wife and himself setting out on life with power and direction. In the background of the picture, on the right, there was a splendid golden sun and on the left a large smoking volcano. We talked of the fact that when we accept our parents as real people who have made their contribution we also accept ourselves as parents and the volcano is a kind of universal symbol of the warmth and energy of Mother Earth.

Perhaps the most interesting feature of the painting was that the foredecks of the two modern ships were piled with coal which the artist could not explain. We eventually decided that it was a reserve of power and energy for their future life, perhaps contributed by the volcano.

When I show this picture to colleagues they always ask about the significance of the sun. There is no doubt that the sun in dreams is often a transforming symbol, but in this case I think it was also a pun, and that his own son was now a source of brightness in his life rather than an area in which he might be found wanting. This patient also confirmed my hope that psychotherapy does more than merely remove symptoms. He wrote me some time later to say that he had had a vivid dream of a design which he transferred to his drawing board and won an architectural competition.

Some patients seem to live in a constant state of tension and anxiety and their bronchospasm may be their psychological signature tune, especially if there is a family history of asthma. One clergyman had never seen either parent as being fallible and was constantly tense in an attempt to be the good man and the perfect parent to his congregation. He tried hard to deny his shadow side and indeed, any negative qualities in his make-up. We discussed his life style and on his second visit he reported a dream in which he entered my consulting room and on the desk was an old fashioned apothecary's drug chest. In the dream I had asked him to select a drug which would cure his asthma, so he chose a jar and turned it round to see the label which read "SIN"! We worked on the idea that a little mischief might help him to relax. He managed to organise his parish duties so that he could find time to pursue his hobby of music and indeed he composed some very elegant church music. It was interesting that when his asthma improved he had a dream of playing a church organ at full power with all the stops out. Clearly there were no problems with the airways at that stage!

16. Peptic ulcer

*The view that a peptic ulcer may be
the hole in a man's stomach through
which he crawls to escape from his
wife has fairly wide acceptance.*

J A D Anderson

*The devil's ploy is to see that we work
so hard that we do no work at all.*

St Vincent de Paul

Like many other psychosomatic disorders, peptic ulcer is of
relatively recent origin. In the early part of the 20th century
the common manifestation was gastric ulceration mainly
affecting females and often presenting as a perforation. The
incidence of peptic ulcer, and especially that of duodenal
ulcer, has arisen steadily though there is some evidence of a
decline in the past twenty years.

Peptic ulcer has a genetic component and sufferers tend to show other shared genes such as blood groups. Much attention and research has been linked to the secretion of hydrochloric acid from the gastric mucous membrane since peptic ulcer does not occur in patients with no acid secretion. The acid apparently must be present if ulceration is to occur but the actual level is quite variable.

Sinclair-Gieben (33) and his psychiatric colleagues in Aberdeen suggested that peptic ulcer patients fall into two groups. Those with gastric ulcers and a number of those with duodenal ulcers tended to be depressive personalities, while the majority of the duodenal ulcer patients were obsessional strivers, who could nevertheless occasionally become depressed if they failed to achieve their objectives. My colleague Dr Glen (34, 35) then showed that the first group tended to have relatively low levels of acid output and that this was largely controlled by parasympathetic stimuli through the vagus nerve. The obsessional group had high acid output which was not of a vagal origin but which was related to antral and pancreatic stimulation as is seen in its pure form in the Zollinger-Ellison syndrome.

My clinical experience in peptic ulcer has seen many changes in both the medical and surgical attitudes to treatment. When I came upon the medical scene the ulcer patients were confined to bed (on wheels!) and given two hourly milk feeds. Not surprisingly this enforced regression to infancy resulted in frequent bed wetting. The dietary regimes became gradually more enlightened though it is still common to find ulcer patients who avoid fried food only because they are so instructed and not because it produces discomfort.

Modern drugs such as the H2-antagonists are successful in reducing or eliminating acid secretion and provide short term benefit which can be an invaluable adjunct to treatment. It seems likely that we have forgotten that one of the functions of the gastric acid is to kill ingested bacteria and it is now being noticed that ulcer patients have stomachs colonised by organisms such as helicobacter. One wonders whether these are secondary to treatment with acid inhibiting drugs rather than of any causal significance for the ulcer.

The surgical history during my spell as an observer began with the successful treatment of actual perforation of the ulcer, and undoubtedly beneficial management of pyloric narrowing or obstruction by gastro-enterostomy. This involved connecting the stomach to the small bowel lower down and so short-circuiting both the narrowed stomach exit (the pylorus) and the duodenum. Later developments allowed other complications to be treated surgically, with partial removal of the stomach (gastrectomy) offering substantial gains for severe bleeding or in ulcer-cancer. Indeed I have been impressed by how successful and free of later trouble have been the patients who had surgical treatment for these complications of their ulcer. These good results have often obscured the fact that those treated surgically for uncomplicated, albeit severe ulcer dyspepsia, fared much less well in terms of post operative health, an opinion which may not be shared by my surgical colleagues

Gastroenterostomy was commonly offered to these patients with intractable dyspepsia in the early days but was often followed by troublesome complications. On the principle of "if thine eye offend thee ..." there was then a spell, when the surgical treatment was by partial gastrectomy to remove the ulcer-prone areas of the stomach and duodenum. A number of those patients deprived of the refuge of their indigestion, became alcoholics, drug addicts or depressives. The surgeons eventually changed their tactics to devise simpler operations such as vagotomy and pyloroplasty, where the nerve stimulating acid secretion was divided and the stomach outlet was widened. This procedure gave improved results.

For many years my medical clinics were engulfed in post operative problems. One sad depressed man when asked why he wasn't working replied, "I haven't the stomach for the job, doctor!" Another man who had been insistent on having surgical treatment admitted that his hope had been that he would not survive the operation. It is interesting that at no time did I ever hear a word of criticism directed at the surgeons. All the patients were grateful for the skill shown and the effort made. One woman was admitted to our medical ward, dehydrated and emaciated from persistent vomiting following surgery for a duodenal ulcer. After the "fire brigade" work of resuscitation we spent much time talking. She claimed that when a few days old she had been found abandoned on a railway platform and had been adopted by the porter who found her. My own cynical thought was that he was probably her real father but made no such inflammatory comment! When she became an expense around the age of sixteen she was asked to leave the home and developed dyspepsia. Recently she had been abandoned by her husband. Such a catalogue of rejection would make her vomiting predictable. When fit and well and ready to leave hospital she made the fascinating comment, "I'm beginning to feel the benefit of my operation!"

There are, as usual, wide cultural differences in the natural history of ulcer patients. For example, perforated ulcer is relatively uncommon in the United States as compared with Great Britain. There are also sex differences - females often complain less of indigestion but more commonly have reflex oesophageal spasm and present as dysphagia.

The common personality pattern of the duodenal ulcer patient is that of the virtuous obsessional. They tend to describe their family as undemonstrative and can seldom remember sitting on a parent's knee. The home background was strict in terms of cleanliness and punctuality. The excretory functions were a taboo subject or at least shrouded in negative messages so that as in many gastrointestinal disorders the gut was untouchable or at best, of no importance.

Mothers have had to accept a great deal of opprobrium in psychological literature and a small number of ulcer patients had dyspeptic mothers, but in this illness it is wise to look for the father's role. A large majority of ulcer patients had a father who was largely absent during the birth to twelve year old stage. He had died, or there was a divorce or separation, or the father had an occupation which involved long periods away from home at sea, in the armed services, or working abroad. Some were ostensibly at home but often worked in the evening or on emergency call-out. Doctors' children often qualify in this category! Frequently the father had a peptic ulcer and was likely to have qualities that produced behaviour similar to genuine absence.

Ulcer patients, in my experience, are the most dependent group of all psychosomatic sufferers. As they were seldom cuddled and their father was often absent they grow up seeing themselves as untouchable and indeed may feel that they had induced the father's absence by their behaviour. As children their unattainable need to be warmly loved was so great that it had to be denied and they tend to compensate for their feared emotional deficiencies by intellectual and professional success.

Dependency first registers with the infant as the need for regular feeds so it is not surprising that orality is a feature of the ulcer patient. Many are very food conscious and it is common to find that they enjoy symbolic food-stuffs such as milk, mashed potatoes or creamed rice. This dependency may well be a factor in the alcohol problems of some post-operative ulcer patients. Since the key to successful marriage is to accept mutual dependence with gratitude and without embarrassment, marital relationships can be strained if the dependency needs have to be denied. It is noticeable for example that ulcer patients become irritable or indeed angry if their spouse is ill as they feel threatened by this potential loss.

Ulcer patients are also threatened or at least ambivalent about any close emotional relationship. Many develop their symptoms when they become engaged or marry. One of my most promising registrars reported to me that he had seen a young woman with a confirmed duodenal ulcer of six months duration. He said, "She has been engaged for six months and every night she dreams she is being chased through a forest by a huge gorilla. I explained to her that marriage wasn't in the least like that. Was that the right management?"

I once asked a charming acquaintance why she had only one child and she replied, "I couldn't risk it. My husband's ulcer perforated on the day our daughter was born".

Patients with ulcers court isolation as pseudo-independence and choose suitable occupations. In the West of Scotland the commonest occupation among 400 hospital patients was overhead crane-driver, isolated yet controlling. It is easy to see that this front of independence is a screen for dependency needs. One highly successful Trade Union official had a splendid warm spouse, and he admitted that he began to experience epigastric pain if he even left his house to post a letter.

The ulcer personality has advantages and disadvantages. As employees they may be off work occasionally but on the whole are so meticulous and obsessional that this more than compensates. Indeed as household tradesmen they are worth their weight in gold. Ulcer sufferers remain young in emotional development but also in appearance and this has advantages in later life. The disadvantages are mainly that they must maintain their perfectionist goals by always being right, and some go to great and devious lengths to prove someone else to blame for any mishap, so that their families become confused by being used as scapegoats. I recently talked with a self-doubting young woman who described her father as having a lifelong ulcer problem so I asked if he had a need to be right. She replied, "He wasn't always right, but of course he was never wrong!"

Many ulcer patients are surprisingly aggressive and ruthless and are often employed by large firms as the "hatchet man" who does the sackings. Criticism of any kind is particularly threatening and may result in physical complications such as bleeding or perforation, or in emotional reactions in which they rapidly regress to childish and petulant behaviour.

My records of peptic ulcer patients include a number who were considered to have nervous dyspepsia. These had much the same background and personality as the proven ulcer patients and I suspect could have developed true ulceration in the future. 170 patients had psychodynamic interviews and 118 had psychotherapy. The age range was 18-63 (average 44) years and the sex distribution was almost equally divided. 19% of this group claimed to be symtom free after counselling.

For comparison I have included in Appendix TABLE B a group of 46 patients who were seen while reviewing the results of the early trials of vagotomy and pyloroplasty. Three quarters of this group were male, as is more characteristic of ulcer patients. 83% were much improved after surgery though none were totally symptom free. In both the surgical and the psychotherapy groups there were approximately 20% who were unchanged by either treatment.

The post-operative patients were given three questionnaires to complete by a colleague and then had a twenty minute interview with me. This interview tended to confirm my cynical view of questionnaires, with several revealing episodes. One man had noted on the form that his indigestion had started while he was on the Island of Mull. When I asked what had taken him to Mull he replied, "Well, I could hardly write down that I had been in prison at the time".

Peptic ulcer patients are good subjects for psychotherapy and generally co-operate with intelligence and humour. Even with unselected and allocated patients in another large trial the results were reasonable since the rather depressed, low acid type patients, improved physically and also were promoted at work or embarked on having a family. The high acid obsessionals also improved and learned to relax and embarked on new hobbies and other leisure pursuits. In this trial the matched controls were given conventional treatment by surgeons in a peptic ulcer clinic. The trial was somewhat invalidated as the surgeons became so interested in their cohort that they unwittingly began to do their own brand of psychotherapy with their patients!

With most patients the areas which must be explored are their early childhood and the constant theme of absent fathers and emotionally undemonstrative parents. They have to be encouraged to see their gastrointestinal system in a more affectionate and less hostile fashion and to look at the reason for their perfectionistic and obsessional behaviour.

The first patient I attempted to treat by psychotherapy was a charming, highly intelligent and competent staff nurse who had a six months history of dyspepsia and her duodenal ulcer was confirmed radiologically. I was interested that she said that her initial symptoms had coincided with the moment when she had first put on her engagement ring. She was the eldest of her family and had had a fairly strict upbringing. She remembered frequent parental quarrels so that she was not too sure that her own marriage could be successful and was having some problems in non-verbal communication with her fiancé.

As I was inexperienced it took me several weeks to notice that somewhere in her dreams there was almost always the figure of a policeman. When, at last, I asked when she had been involved with the police she said that she had almost forgotten that she had been sexually assaulted at the age of eight. The episode was followed by a medical examination, identity parades and so on. Sex had been thrust upon her too early, and she was immediately able to relate this to her apprehension regarding her marriage. She then had a dream that she was in a prison camp and a guard pointed a revolver at her but she knew it wasn't going to harm her and could ignore it. Her final dream was sharing a car with her fiancé and a nursing colleague. She had slightly disapproved of this nurse in real life as she regarded her as too sexy! In the dream they drove along and she gradually merged with the other nurse. The car stopped on a bridge and she and her fiancé leapt over into the river (of life) and swam off happily together.

At our next interview she offered her fiancé's dream that they were on their honeymoon and he had found his suitcase was empty. I had not yet learned the subtleties of ending therapy but I felt that my patient was in danger of outgrowing her future husband, who now felt threatened and slightly inadequate, so we parted company. A further x-ray showed no evidence of ulcer.

Another young patient had probably the poorest self esteem I have ever encountered. She was twenty-one when first seen and had a four years history of severe epigastric pain with bouts of vomiting suggesting pylorospasm. A barium meal showed only pylorospasm. She attended regularly as an outpatient and never missed an appointment but spent the time abusing me for not being more helpful. She claimed that she never dreamt so it was difficult to assess her problems. She asserted that her twin sister, who was fit and happily married, had always been the favourite and so she felt inadequate. However my role as the "bad" father was so obvious that when confronted with this she admitted that there had been attempts at incest. She felt disreputable as a result and this explained her poor self image. The patient was encouraged to leave home and for a spell improved but when she returned home she again had pain and vomiting. Then a minor miracle occurred. She went to stay with her sister and her four year old niece climbed onto her knee; flung tiny arms round her neck and said, "You're such a lovely auntie". She suddenly realised that she was not an unloveable failure.

My only further contact was a letter describing her happy married life and the birth of her first child.

I tended to tease my surgical colleagues about their mechanistic approach to ulcer patients and one responded by referring a man whom he claimed could only be helped by surgery. The patient was pitifully thin and miserable. He was an insurance agent but also a lay preacher. With this interest in his heavenly father I asked about his earthly father. He apparently was the villain of the piece who had deserted the patient and his mother many years previously. His initial dreams were encouraging as he was scraping paint and stripping wallpaper to see what was underneath, and then he had a nice earthy dream of helping his wife to weed the garden and had found a snake plant. With some embarrassment he said, "And we all know what snakes mean". I assured him that snakes were important long before Freud. They were the medical symbol that man and not only God could sometimes heal us. I suggested that he write a sermon on the wisdom of the serpent which allowed Adam and Eve to escape from the intra-uterine life of the Garden of Eden and to have the reward of being allowed to work and to bear children. Shortly thereafter he became free of pain and began to gain weight. He had one further bout of dyspepsia on receiving a letter from his father but he remembered our discussions and arranged a meeting with his father which was amicable and helpful. My surgical colleague was almost approving when he saw his patient had gained twelve kilograms in weight.

There is undoubtedly a point at which surgical treatment is mandatory as in patients with continual blood loss from chronic ulceration. One such patient steadfastly refused surgery and was moved to our medical ward for review. He was chronically anaemic so one hoped for a speedy solution. In the first interview he was asked about his objections to surgical treatment and I found that his wife had undergone a gastroenterostomy and had died post-operatively. So we explored his fear and also his anger and mistrust of surgeons generally. The patient had recurring nightmares of being in an operating theatre where the staff all changed into predatory animals. He was an extremely fastidious man with, at home, a complicated routine of ablutions. Very soon he reported a dream in which he was walking along a city street carrying a frying pan covered by a piece of newspaper. He said, "The paper in the pan blew away and it was full of sausages". It seemed that he was perhaps talking about a bed pan and it seemed likely that his own intestinal canal was no longer totally untouchable. His final recorded dream was that he was again walking but on this occasion with a black spaniel on a lead on his left side. We discussed the possibility that his anger and other negative feelings were now represented by an animal which was under control and no longer threatening. The patient then had his operation and a few weeks later the surgeon reported, "You remember that difficult nervous chap who was refusing surgery. Well, he recovered from his operation faster than any other patient I can remember".

Since the ulcer patients tend to be unusually clean and tidy it is not surprising that they may have psycho-sexual problems but it is wise to regard these merely as a barometer of their general wellbeing rather than as a primary problem.

To conclude I would like to describe a fragment of therapy which is intriguing because it is difficult to explain as are all the most interesting things. The patient was a highly successful scientist with a duodenal ulcer confirmed by both radiology and endoscopy. He felt so ill that he had come to an emotional standstill. Indeed he was almost literally motionless, being unable to work or communicate with his wife or children. He soon described a dream in which he had left a test tube on his laboratory bench and when he returned to collect it there was a large label attached to the test tube and on the label was the word "Lumella". I asked if he had done Latin at school and found that his education had only

been sciences and that he had never attempted any languag
study. I promised to look up the word in my Latin dictionar
and was unable to find it. So I had to beg help from one of m
more erudite friends and eventually the word was found i
the oldest list of Latin vocabulary in the Bodleian Library i
Oxford. It had fallen out of use some 500-1000 BC and was
leather thong used to immobilise slaves by tying their ankle
together. This was an accurate comment on my patient'
present state but it is fascinating to speculate whether th
word had somehow remained in his genetic equipment fo
some 3000 years..

17 Inflammatory bowel disease

*Ye are not straitened in us, but ye are
straitened in your own bowels.*

2 Corinthians 6: 12

Under this heading I propose to offer my views on ulcerative colitis and Crohn's Disease. It is interesting, if only for historical importance, to note that the latter disease has changed over the years. In my undergraduate and early post graduate experience Crohn's Disease was also known as Regional Ileitis and presented with the clinical picture of mid-gut sub-acute obstruction (Crohn et al (36,37)). A sausage-like palpable mass was often obvious running transversely in the right iliac fossa and the disease appeared to be confined to the terminal ileum.

Crohn's as an eponym is widely recognised, though th condition was described much earlier and very clearly by Glasgow surgeon, Sir Kennedy Dalziel. The Universit Pathology Museum in my old hospital has the origin specimen on show. In the 1940s I spent some time in Ne York and was puzzled to be shown cases of Crohn's Diseas which I would have regarded as fairly typical of ulcerativ colitis. But over the 1950s the picture changed in the Unite Kingdom and the two conditions appeared to merge and wer often difficult to differentiate either clinically or histologicall For practical purposes we know that ulcerative colitis confine itself to the colon, while Crohn's Disease may produce "skip lesions" affecting any part of the intestinal canal from th tongue southwards and for this reason is a much mor difficult condition to treat. Both conditions have th unpleasant complication of polyarthropathy. Antibodies t colonic tissue are sometimes found in inflammatory bowe disease and this auto-immune response could perhaps be th biological equivalent of "hating one's guts"!

There was a spell in the 1950s and 1960s when I claimed to be able to distinguish between the two conditions by the psychodynamic and social background of the patients but this aspect also appeared to merge as time passed. In the early 1970s I interviewed a series of patients who were awaiting surgery for inflammatory bowel disease without being told the diagnosis. I found almost similar background detail, and was quite unable to make a valid differentiation on their history. Dr John W Paulley (38, 39, 40) who has a vast experience of gastrointestinal disorders has written of differentiating points in his patients which are much more detailed and sophisticated than my rather crude investigations.

To understand some of the possible mechanism of colitis it is perhaps worth trying to simplify some of the theory of anal aggression. When the infant first becomes aware of his own capacity to empty his bowel at twelve to eighteen months, he ealises that this has involved some hard work and indeed regards it as his day's work. He will show some dismay if the product is flushed away without being admired. But at this stage the power is undifferentiated and must include negative feelings as if his power could be aggressive enough to injure his loved ones. The next time the child asserts himself could be depicted by the scenario in which he refuses to eat some of his meal. His mother will say, "Right, I'll get on with my work and come back when you have finished". The mother leaves the room but the child registers only that he had made his mother disappear and for all he knows she may have died. So to assert oneself is highly dangerous. The child will then only sit on his potty if his mother is actually present and preferably holding a hand.

Alternatively he becomes constipated to avoid using this dangerous power or develops diarrhoea so that no effort is involved - and this is probably a related need in ulcerative colitis patients. Most children experience this type of reaction as a fairly trivial and transient phase. That defaecation can be a manifestation of anger will be obvious to any observant dog owner and so is probably a valid human response and not merely a psychological theory.

It appears that to some extent the colon represents the "evil eye" and in colonic disorders it is important to investigate how the patients deal with their anger. Many ulcerative colitis patients believe they have been responsible for someone's death and Paulley has described how these patients tend to walk away from domestic confrontations. One of my ulcerative colitis patients whose father and brother had died actually stated, "I sin with my eyes".

The first patient whom I looked at in depth developed ulcerative colitis at the age of nineteen. To summarise the story, she described how when she was seven she had asked her mother for a ballet frock. Her mother had said they could not afford it and the disappointed child said, "I wish you were dead and father would buy me a frock". Within a month the mother developed acute leukaemia and died. The child would certainly repress the incident but at nineteen her fiance died of peritonitis. The second death was followed by the onset of her colitis and this is a familiar pattern in this disorder. The patient's colitis cleared up with psychotherapy and I followed her up for twenty-five years without a relapse.

Many ulcerative colitis patients need surgery especially as long standing disease can be complicated by colonic cancer. Emergency surgery may be essential in patients who develop acute toxic megacolon. Patients with Crohn's Disease may also require surgery. When a colectomy is indicated it is likely that patients who have a very fastidious personality will resent their ileostomy and its care and control. These people may benefit by short term psychotherapy to help them to overcome this problem. However, many patients with either of these disorders may be controlled by medical treatment including the use of cortisone type steroids.

My series of ulcerative colitis comprises 53 patients aged 13 to 68 (average 33) years, of whom 42 had psychotherapy of an average duration of 20 months. I have only ten cases of Crohn's Disease aged 15 to 70 (average 26) years of whom eight had psychotherapy for an average time of four months. The Crohn's Disease patients tended to have mainly supportive psychotherapy.

One of the patients, previously mentioned, whom I interviewed before his operation was aged 26 and his story was that when he was seven years old he and his mother went to a cinema. On their return the front door was jammed shut and could not be opened. There was only one small window open so the lad climbed in and found his father lying dead behind the front door. One year before I saw him his mother had died and he then developed frequent loose stools. This story was so typical that I confidently diagnosed ulcerative colitis but in fact he had Crohn's Disease confirmed by the subsequent operation.

At one stage our hospital physicians attempted a properly organised trial of ulcerative colitis stringently planned by our statisticians. All the patients were confirmed cases of ulcerative colitis and all were on a standard regime of treatment and it was planned that they should all be reviewed by totally independent observers. Half the patients were to have psychotherapy in addition to the standard regime. My senior registrar and I were initially allocated two patients each.

I shall summarise one as an example. A thirty year old engineer had a five years history of ulcerative colitis. The illness had started abruptly with ten blood-stained stools a day while he was on holiday with his wife and family in Fife on the East coast of Scotland. The patient had been in hospital at the age of two following a severe dog bite and to some extent he equated illness with punishment. His upbringing had been rigid and he described his mother as "fussy". At the age of twelve his mother suspected her husband of philandering and the patient was sent by the mother to follow his father around and report his movements and meetings. He was caught in an acute dilemma of divided loyalties and was extremely miserable. When his father left home a couple of years later the lad felt guilty and responsible. His father subsequently re-married and was then living in FIFE. Not a very difficult therapeutic problem and he improved rapidly. After a period of three months, our four patients had mild constipation as their only complaint, so mysteriously there was a sudden shortage of patients for treatment and no more could be found! An amusing but rather sad end to the trial.

Many of the histories of ulcerative colitis victims are studded with death and disaster. One thirty-two year old woman had a five years history of colitis. When she was aged two her younger sister was born and her father at that point left home and was never seen again. She then lived with her maternal grandmother and shared her bedroom. The grandmother was both verbally and physically abusive and the young girl was often both afraid and angry. When she was twelve she awoke one day to find that her grandmother had died during the night and she felt guilty that she had not been awake to help her. The patient was a very successful secretary and became engaged to a student. By dint of working for two firms at once she helped him through university, and when he graduated they married and emigrated. Two months after the marriage her husband went out one afternoon to buy some ice cream and failed to return (c.f. father). He was eventually found to have died of a heart attack on his way back to the house. She coped with the funeral without shedding a tear and returned to Britain. On the first anniversary of her husband's funeral she developed diarrhoea with blood, mucus and pus. It was two years before she could open the trunks she had brought home and when she did so she developed angio-oedema of her face. Only then was the patient able to weep for her husband.

I was occasionally horrified by the insensitivity of my elders and betters in the profession. One young patient had severe ulcerative colitis and when she was about to be married her fiance was summoned to the hospital and was instructed on how to give a nightly prednisolone enema to his wife on the honeymoon. What a romantic start to married life! Not surprisingly the patient developed sexual difficulties and the husband became impotent. When I saw her some years later she made a quite inordinate fuss about having a vene-puncture so it was not difficult to ask the correct questions and the story unfolded. By sheer instinct I asked if the needle reminded her of anything else. The lady recalled an episode from around the age of four when her mother was quite seriously ill and she was forbidden to enter her bedroom. She must have felt that this confirmed her fears that she was responsible for her mother's illness. She was extremely upset and her father thrashed her with a cane for showing emotion. After spending some time with both partners it was interesting and probably significant that their parting present was a wrought iron fireside poker decorated with a ram's head!

Occasionally ulcerative colitis may originate as a more direct outcome of trauma. One lady had made a disastrous marriage to a man who insisted on having anal intercourse. Her first symptoms occurred while she was giving evidence in the divorce court.

My final case history started unusually in that I was invited to see a patient in the professorial medical unit where, as you can imagine, pure science normally had all the answers! To ask a hack physician from another medical unit was surprising but the reason was entirely admirable in that the patient was such a charming fellow that they wanted to leave no stone, even psychological stones, unturned. The patient was a thirty-five year old engineering manager who had only recently come to Scotland from the South of England, from an area which prides itself on its expertise on ulcerative colitis. He was married with two children and had an eighteen months history of severe ulcerative colitis. While in the South he had had fourteen sigmoidoscopies (instrumental examinations) in one year! He was the youngest of four siblings and when he was thirteen his parents separated. He felt that someone must stay and help his father so he undertook the household chores after his day at school. He said that when he was fifteen, his father had been killed in a road accident and he returned to live with his mother. He trained as an engineer and was highly successful in his career. In his twenties while walking home from work he encountered a young nurse whose cycle had a puncture. He repaired the puncture and she eventually became his wife. They moved to Scotland as he was appointed to a highly responsible job and was very honoured to be asked to lecture to engineering students.

"But," I asked, "What happened when your colitis started?"

He replied, "No one ever asked me that question. I went up to say goodnight to my youngest daughter and she was dead in her cot". Fourteen sigmoidoscopies as a treatment for bereavement! So I harked back to father's death. "It wasn't a road accident was it?" In fact the boy had unexpectedly been asked to play football for his school and came home two hours later than normal to find his father had committed suicide. He felt he was responsible for his father's death and when his daughter died the second death had precipitated the illness.

At first, like many men, he was reluctant to admit to dreaming but finally volunteered a dream that he had been driving his car accompanied by his wife. She had pulled on the handbrake and it fell off. I asked if he was preparing a lecture for his students and he agreed that this was so. "And is your wife complaining that you're not making love to her?" - Of course! He was then able to accept that dreams might occasionally mean something and began to make progress. As befits a very intelligent man who used his work as a defence he began by dreaming he was on the top of high cranes controlling things, but gradually began to climb down ladders and eventually to dream that he was laying black asphalt on his driveway, which suggested that his stools were becoming formed. Later when much improved he had a dream that he was swimming in a London dock in filthy water with pieces of moss floating about. I suggested that, rather than swimming, he was going through the motions and that his bowel was no longer untouchable and no longer an enemy, and so indeed it was. I knew the patient was now nearly ready to stop attending, but I feared that he might see this as killing off yet another father.

However, on his next visit he had a fairly normal sexy dream of manoeuvering a submarine into a slipway in a dockyard and said to himself "I can manage this on my own. I wish that commander would stop telling me what to do". I was intrigued that his unconscious should have correctly guessed my former naval rank and I reckoned that he no longer needed my help, so we agreed that his next visit should be the final one. On the occasion of his last visit he reported a dream that he had been walking along a city street and met a beautiful lady whose bicycle had a flat tyre. He told her she needed a new inner tube and went to a shop nearby and bought it. The salesman said, "You know how to fit it and look after it now". So he had a new colon and I knew that I might get another message that I was superfluous to his requirements, so I asked him who the salesman was. "That's funny, it was the professor of medicine!"

The patient telephoned me the following May to say he had mild diarrhoea. We chatted and it settled, but a year later he telephoned with the same story. I was puzzled as his father had died in January and the daughter in August so if it was an anniversary reaction why in this particular month. I had a flash of intuition and asked the daughter's name - May. So each time he wrote the date he was being reminded, and that insight appeared to complete the recovery.

18. Irritable bowel syndrome

Not only degrees of pain, but its existence,
in any degree, must be taken upon the
testimony of the patient.

Peter Mere Latham

Irritable bowel syndrome is an extremely common condition and is often in danger of becoming a diagnostic dustbin for anyone who complains of abdominal pain. It seems possible that many of the population develop some degree of the condition in the second half century of their lives, but how they are "inconvenienced" depends on many other factors. It is vitally important to avoid diagnostic errors varying from colonic malignancy at one end of the spectrum to conditions such as magacolon, atonic colon or endometriosis at the other.

À careful history is mandatory and often diagnostic and the presence of palpable spasm of the sigmoid region is helpful. Barium enema may show actual spasm or the presence of diverticuli, though often the X-ray is within normal limits. The patient may present with diverticulitis and if there is diverticular inflammation, the complications of fistula formation into the bladder or other areas may arise. Repeated local inflammation may result in fibrous stricture of the colon and it is reassuring, if obstruction occurs, to expect simple fibrous narrowing rather than malignant disease. These patient tend to have a hypersensitive gastrointestinal canal and often have hypermotility, or dyspepsia with at times peptic ulceration or oesophageal regurgitation. This phenomenon is confirmed by the changing labels applied to the condition from the early descriptions of mucous colitis or spastic colon to irritable colon syndrome and finally irritable bowel syndrome. While the condition is most common in middle life it may occur in the late teens or twenties. Halliday believed that disorders with a psychosomatic component tended to affect ever younger groups as time passes.

It would seem that the initial internal fist clenching occurs in the sigmoid region. The resultant increased pressure locally is probably a factor in the formulation of diverticuli and the back pressure effect causes distention of the splenic and hepatic flexures or the caecal area, with considerable resultant discomfort.

It has long been known that writer's cramp could be helped by using a very thick pencil as if limiting the degree of flexion prevented the final spasm and cramp. A similar mechanism may account for the benefit derived from a high fibre diet by distending the bowel lumen and inhibiting spasm.

The emotional component in this group of patients is less specific than in many other psychosomatic conditions though the features described in the previous chapter on inflammatory bowel disease are often present, if in a less strident fashion. Many are fastidious and obsessional and in their childhood had parents who insisted on a weekly dose of "syrup of figs" regardless of its requirement. Many develop symptoms after bereavement and many have difficulty in expressing anger verbally.

The fear of an explosive bowel movement may initiate an overwhelming crisis as they rise to make a speech or to give a lecture or in broadcasters as the second hand of the studio clock approaches their scripted moment. Any relaxation technique may be helpful in such patients and psychotherapy can make a contribution though the results are much less spectacular than in more threatening illnesses such as ulcerative colitis. My series comprises 120 patients aged 14 to 67 (average 35.6) years of whom 100 had psychotherapy of an average duration of 18 months. 71% were considered to be obsessional And 62% had an episode of bereavement or separation.

A thirty-five year old man was admitted to hospital with a five to six year's history of intermittent abdominal pain with bouts of diarrhoea, occasionally passing mucus and blood. The symptoms started during his engagement and he had been married for five years. The patient was the youngest of a large family and his father had died of colonic cancer when he was nine years old. The upbringing was strict and fundamentalist religion was highly important in the household. He had always been fastidious and obsessed with cleanliness so that his illness was embarrassing as well as painful. On his second interview he was encouraged to go back in time and discuss his father's illness and death. He gradually became aware of the fact that, as the youngest son, he had tried to replace father and to give extra support to his widowed mother. It was suggested that he might have felt disloyal to his mother when he became engaged and to this he readily agreed and felt he ought to be punished. The Talion Law appears to have been involved in that his suffering had to resemble that of his father whom he felt he was betraying. At this stage he had been having a recurrent nightmare of being stuck in concrete but the dreams soon changed to activity as in dreams of playing football. After discussion of his need for cleanliness he had a more promising dream of driving a tractor which became stuck in mud and he fell off into the mud without any feelings of apprehension or revulsion. After six days in hospital his bowel was normal and pain-free and he stated, "I see the world bright again". Shortly after this he dreamt he was rowing a small boat in a very stormy sea but managed to reach his destination safely. So it seemed likely he would cope with life's difficulties fairly successfully. A chance encounter twenty years later confirmed that there had been no relapse.

My next example was unusual in that I was asked to see a forty-five year old man after he had received pre-medication for an exploratory operation. The surgeon had suddenly second thoughts. The story was suggestive of intermittent bouts of irritable bowel syndrome and perhaps under the influence of the sedative he told me that his attacks always started when his mother came to visit the family. So the operation was abandoned and we agreed to talk for a few weeks and see what transpired. He was a delightful and successful man who could easily have been university material. He was a technician in a a hospital pathology department and spent much of his time teaching junior medical and technical staff. He saw his mother as infallible but she was, in fact, a somewhat intimidating and domineering lady. The turning point of the patient's therapy was when he had a dream of looking for something at home and he opened a storage cupboard under the staircase. His mother fell out of the cupboard dressed in disreputable old clothes and covered with cobwebs. So, mother was no longer infallible and his symptoms slowly subsided over a couple of months. When he was well and no longer requiring psychotherapeutic help he provided a pleasant confirmation of this by dreaming that he invented a new staining process and on examining the slide under the microscope he could see everything clearly and was congratulated by his pathologist. We agreed to part company and as he left I said, "By the way, what was the tissue you stained so cleverly?" and he replied, "Breast". Much laughter ensued.

I shall conclude this chapter with a further example to illustrate the variability of the psychological background. The patient was a thirty-five year old woman who was admitted to hospital with an eighteen months history of abdominal pain and irregular bowel function. She had been thoroughly investigated elsewhere and the diagnosis was confirmed but she had not improved on treatment.

The family history was that her father had been on active service in the Second World War and was seldom at home. He was invalided from the services when she was twelve on account of a duodenal ulcer and subsequently had a gastroenterostomy and later a partial gastrectomy. Her elder brother also had a peptic ulcer. The mother had bronchitis and the younger brother suffered from asthma.

The early years sounded difficult. The patient's mother was probably struggling to cope with three children on her own and was strict and undemonstrative in terms of physical affection. Any attempt at independence or rebellion was frowned upon and the patient said, "My temper was beaten out of me". Father was a gentler individual with whom the patient identified though he tended to be possessive and, in later years, disapproved of her male friends. When the West of Scotland had its share of air raids the two brothers were sent away to live with relatives in a safer area. It was during this spell of separation that her brother developed asthma. She felt she was kept at home as it was more important that the boys should be safe. This bizarre episode was probably for some very sensible reason, but it left the patient with a feeling that females were less valuable.

The patient had never had any long term relationship with men and tended to be the one who ended the relationship and one such occasion occurred at the start of her illness. On admission the patient had told the house physician that she had no intention of marrying or of having children. Her progress in psychotherapy was somewhat spasmodic though fortunately she had a lively sense of humour. We worked on her identity and especially her male-female role and she would say things like, "The pain comes back as soon as I begin to feel cocky again". She seemed to improve but relapsed on returning to her parents' home and required re-admission. It was likely that some part of the psychological jigsaw puzzle was missing and this seemed to be confirmed by a dream in two parts. In the first half of the dream she felt that the cause of the illness was unknown and that she must wait and see, and in the second half of the same dream she felt that she might try writing down her ideas or perhaps find someone other than myself to whom she could talk. After a weekend at home she asked if I would telephone her family doctor and when I did so this unusually sensitive man told me that he had the patient's permission to report on her visit to him. She had told him of an attempted sexual assault at the age of eight. So we discussed her feelings of disgust and of being unclean and of the inevitable impression that it was all her fault and that she must have provoked the incident. It seemed likely that her recurrent diarrhoea was an attempt to "get rid of the dirt" and she certainly had little affection for her gut. She improved rapidly and exactly one year after her first admission she announced that she now liked men and was married the following year.

19. Psycho-sexual problems

Marriages are not normally made to avoid children.

Rudolph Virchow

It seems most likely that most problems in the psycho-sexual area are dealt with by the family doctor or are referred to the psychiatric services. The physician is more likely to be consulted if some physical or endocrine abnormality is a possibility. Of course, many illnesses both psychosomatic and truly organic have upsets of libido and of emotional relationships as a secondary effect and these usually resolve as the primary condition improves.

My small series of twenty-five patients all had psychotherapy for relatively short times (average nine months) and, indeed, the problems were seldom difficult to solve. The commonest finding was that the patient's parents had an understandable (and very British) embarrassment regarding any mention of

sexual activity or attitudes. The resultant "taboo" tended to
persist but was fairly easily resolved by open and frank
discussion. Many patients were referred by gynaecologists.
One such colleague ran a highly efficient and effective clinic
for infertile couples. She tended to refer the husband to me
when no physical abnormality had been found in either
spouse. The majority of such referrals involved people, often
of strict upbringing or for other reasons, who had long been
indoctrinated that they had a duty to produce children. This
attitude of mechanistic determination was not likely to be
either enjoyable or effective. One or two talks on the priority
of recreation over procreation and a general discussion on
love-making as an art form, usually resulted in a telephone
call from my colleague asking, "What did you say to that man
- his wife is pregnant".

Many years ago I was intrigued to note that a female patient
had been referred by an anaesthetist. He reported that he had
been about to anaesthetise her for a dilatation and curettage
when he realised that he had done so only three weeks earlier.
His questioning had revealed that she had undergone ten
such operations in the previous eighteen months under the
care of different gynaecologists, but had omitted to choose her
anaesthetists so carefully. It seemed obvious that she had a
great need to have her feminity scraped away. She was a twin
and in her infancy her parents had found the load too heavy
and had handed her over to the care of her grandparents, but
had kept the male twin. As I was a learner at that stage, I
asked a psychiatric colleague to see her. His treatment was
rapidly successful. Confirmation that she no longer needed to
be male reached my home later on, in the form of a splendid
symbolic present of one cucumber and two tomatoes!!

Another patient was referred to exclude the possibility of an
over-active thyroid. Investigation showed her thyroid
function to be normal but it seemed likely that she had an
anxiety state. When asked if she had nightmares, she stated
that she frequently dreamt there was a dead man lying beside

er. "Could it be that you are telling me your husband is
npotent?" I asked, and she replied in some astonishment, "Is
iat why I feel like this?"

A psychoanalyst referred one man who was suffering from
>tal secondary impotence, no doubt aggravated by his wife's
>ng-standing illness which was being treated by my
olleague. This was early on in my own career and I had a
inking feeling that I was being challenged or at least
ssessed. My heart sank even further when I found that the
>atient was a mathematician, but after some preliminary
discussions he began to dream and described a vivid dream
sequence involving the most complicated mathematical
problems. Over a series of dreams he solved the problems
and equations. I had no idea what was going on or what he
was solving but I felt that my understanding was probably
irrelevant. Finally he had a non-mathematical dream of
sitting in the House of Commons with his feet perched up on
the Dispatch Box. "You mean you are able to have an erection
again?" And so it was, and I had learnt another lesson in the
strange process of psychotherapy.

One young woman whose marriage had not been
consummated was a gynaecological referral and the story was
straightforward. Her mother had died at her birth and she
had been brought up by elderly grandparents. Her feminine
identity was tenuous and she felt that she should be punished
for causing her mother's death and this would be in the form
of retaliation in that she would die if she became pregnant.
We had a one hour discussion and about a week later she
telephoned to say, "Isn't sex wonderful!"

One amusing episode occurred when a lady came to see me
after a fifteen years gap. She had been seen earlier with
migraine, but on this occasion she was upset as both her
family doctor and her husband had decided that she was
frigid. She was a warm feminine and slightly untidy person
and my strong impression was that this diagnostic

assumption was untrue. As we talked it became apparent that her husband's business was going through a bad patch and his problems were compounded by two highly rebellious teenage sons who were making their father's life even more difficult. It was soon obvious that the unfortunate husband was suffering from premature ejaculation. We arranged to meet again in a week's time and she then announced, "After our last talk I went off walking on air as it was not all my fault, so I went home and had a nice helpful chat with my husband about his shortcomings!"

I shall summarise two final histories which were undertaken in a somewhat experimental fashion to assess whether psychotherapy could influence hormonal function.

A twenty-nine year old female came to consult me primarily about feelings of depression and failure. At the age of twenty-one she had been found to have pelvic tuberculosis and a pan-hysterectomy had been carried out. We spent several months working through her resentment at this devastating, if necessary, mutilation. Her father had severe pulmonary tuberculosis and she was angry that he was the probable source of infection.   She was also angry with the gynaecologist who had not explained adequately the reasons for her surgery, and who had failed to discuss the implications or to give her time to adjust to the idea. The patient had not had any form of hormone replacement therapy and she agreed to postpone that possibility meantime. As she felt "neutered" she tended to avoid male company and this attitude was partly due to the areas of resentment previously described. She was not a prolific dreamer but her dreams began to show her in more feminine roles and eventually she could dream of having children and of being able to mother them. Despite the fact that she had no hormone replacement she reported after six months that her bust measurement had increased by several inches. She became engaged and was able to share her childless state with her fiancé and to discuss possible adoption in a realistic fashion.

he second psychotherapeutic trial was at the specific request of a gynaecologist who could find no physical reason why a twenty-four year old had never menstruated. When this patient was seven her mother had been admitted to hospital with tuberculosis and remained in hospital until her death eight years later. There was a younger sister and my patient had acted as mother as well as sister and was thrust into adult responsibilities at a very early age. Her father was supportive and helpful but often devastated by his wife's illness. The patient had had almost no opportunity of identifying with her mother or of acquiring a feminine role. We talked at great length about her fears that she was in some way responsible for her mother's illness and discussed how different her childhood might have been had her mother been fit and well. As in the case of the previous patient her dreams began to offer her reassurance of her femininity. After about six months she began to have a slight vaginal discharge in a monthly cycle and by the end of a year she had made a suitable and stable relationship and became engaged. About a month before the date of her marriage she had a normal menstrual period.

20. Negative diagnosis

Errors of judgement must occur in
the practice of an art which consists
largely in balancing probabilities.

William Osler

It has always been advocated that a diagnosis of neurotic or "functional" symptoms should be based on adequate evidence of emotional stress and not merely upon the absence of verifiable physical disease. The converse of this is that an attempt to exclude an emotional component can help to confirm that a clinical problem is in fact organic and should be treated accordingly. I have used the term negative diagnosis to describe these cases where an emotional component should be excluded.

An interest in psychosomatic disease becomes known to one's colleagues and opinion is sought to help to clarify such diagnostic challenges. This type of consultation is often difficult and the answer may still be one of continued dubiety. But there is no doubt that a successful contribution to the diagnostic dilemma is remarkably impressive to one's colleagues and helps greatly in encouraging acceptance of a psychosomatic approach.

Clearly General Practitioners make this type of differentiation many times each day, with remarkable success based upon clinical acumen combined with experience and intuition.

Many direct referrals from family doctors over the past ten years have been for advice on patients showing anxiety, depression and lassitude. The history shows that their previous life style has been successful socially, emotionally, and professionally and that the complaint was often precipitated by a transient febrile illness. Investigation often reveals that their symptoms are due to a post viral syndrome, many attributable to infection by the coxackie group of viruses, which have been endemic in the West of Scotland. The patients are reassured and helped by knowing that there is an organic cause for their illness and though no specific treatment can be offered they are clearly relieved to be considered "non-neurotic".

Some patients are referred as they have themselves decided that they are neurotic. One such thirty year old patient was anorexic, emaciated and depressed. Even a short history showed her to be totally stable emotionally and it was obvious that the illness was organic. A diagnosis of malabsorption syndrome was reached and her self styled neurosis was banished by a gluten-free diet.

Another patient aged forty was referred by a surgical colleague who had noted that his abdominal pain had begun at the time of his wife's death. He had, however, coped well with his bereavement. He had mourned and shared the loss with his children and had reorganised their life and routine in an exemplary fashion. The patient clearly had mid-gut colic so I suggested an operation and a small bowel carcinoma was successfully removed.

One remarkable example of this type of problem was initiated by a surgeon who asked me to see a young woman in his ward as he proposed to operate upon her the following day and had suddenly felt some doubt about this decision. The girl had almost life long bouts of vomiting. X-ray investigations had been negative and this episode was before the era of flexible endoscopy instruments. Despite the attacks of vomiting she had a good school and athletic record and worked as a secretary to a civil engineering firm. She worked on the building sites and enjoyed putting on her wellington boots and trudging around in the mud to find the engineers. None of this suggested the over-fastidious personality one associates with functional vomiting so I offered my opinion that the operation should proceed. She was found to have a congenital duodenal diaphragm with only a pin hole aperture, which of course allowed the liquid barium to pass but was easily obstructed by foodstuffs.

My final example of negative diagnosis concerns a thirty year old lady who had been thoroughly, indeed aggressively, investigated in another city for recurrent bouts of abdominal pain. No diagnosis had been reached and it had been implied that she was neurotic. My initial impression was that she was having genuine attacks of abdominal colic, but I decided that a period of observation was justified as she had a history of childhood asthma, so we met regularly and the story gradually unfolded. At each visit I examined her abdomen and she talked on the couch thereafter. She had been brought up abroad and at the age of seven had gone to a children's holiday camp in the South where she had especially enjoyed picking oranges from the trees. On returning home she found that her parents had separated, and thereafter she developed asthma whenever her mother made marmalade!

At the age of seventeen the patient met her father again and they had an adult conversation about his marriage and the asthma ceased. The only residual hang up was that she avoided any emotional involvement as she felt divorce was inevitable. This seemed a great pity as she was outstandingly attractive and feminine. Several times as we talked she had pain and rumbling relieved by passing wind, so I returned her to the surgeons who carried out an operation and found that she had intermittent small bowel obstruction from a volvulus. Some months later she returned for one further visit to tell me that she had become engaged, but also to say she had had one bout of asthma. She had been staying with friends and their cat had jumped on her lap and she began to wheeze. "And I'm not allergic to cats," she insisted, so I replied, "But it was a marmalade cat!" "My goodness," she replied, "It's name was Chivers!"

21. Terminal illness

*Nature is a benevolent old hypocrite, she cheats
the sick and the dying with illusions better than
any anodynes.*

Oliver Wendel Holmes

*It is foolish to waste lamentations upon the closing
phase of human life. Noble spirits yield themselves
willingly to the successively falling shades.*

Winston Churchill

Our attitudes to death, bereavement and mourning have been
greatly helped in recent years by many outstanding
publications and by the growth of the hospice movement. It
may be merely presumption to make any contribution to this
subject, but I feel that one of the key factors which has not
been sufficiently emphasised is the importance of denial and
the need to assess its influence in each individual case.

Denial is so universal in this area that it is seldom even
noticed. If I have to tell a husband that his wife has just died
he will inevitably say, "No". Instantaneous denial - and this
mechanism dominates the subsequent events. The coffin is

carefully upholstered so that the dead will not be uncomfortable; we speak in whispers at the funeral lest we disturb the most important participant. Even doctors, who should know better, hurry past the bed containing the moribund patient - denial compounded by guilt at our failure to cure.

Perhaps we should consider the origins of this denial. Children are protected by a universal built-in denial mechanism that death is impossible for those upon whom they depend and for themselves. Consequently they cry if a balloon bursts and may say that it has died, as it is not vital to their existence; yet they play at shooting father and if he feigns dead they laugh - he is too important to be regarded as capable of dying. This denial is designed to protect the child for the first fifteen years or so but the denial often persists into adult life. Occasionally there is a rude shock for the child if a parent or a close friend dies. The reality of this bereavement, the bewildered angry abandonment and rejection are repressed, but remain as an unexploded bomb to cause trouble later on. Children who have been fortunate enough to have pets learn to cope with bereavement. They feel sad but usually less guilty than with human death and they learn that eventually they recover and feel happy again. This is invaluable experience for important losses in later life.

In the normal course of events the youngster of sixteen or so encounters death of a grandparent or some such relative and then begins to realise that some day he too will die. At first this is a frightening and indeed a threatening discovery and so he will tend to feel angry. The youngsters should be allowed to talk about this with parents or other listeners or they will become anxious at the potential death of their parents or friends or of themselves. If allowed to discuss the matter they see that there is no need to worry about potential problems and when they meet death it will be a reality and we can all cope with reality. They realise they must accept the mathematical certainty of eventual death and can plan to have lots of fun between here and the cemetery.

It is difficult if not impossible to deal correctly with the terminally ill unless one has first come to terms with our own mortality. I have often discussed death with medical students and I was surprised how often, by the age of twenty or so, they had not yet faced this problem. One group became very angry and retaliated by demanding to know how I wanted to die - a difficult question - the only reply I could muster was that I hoped that at the age of ninety I would be shot by a jealous husband. The delightful sequel to this teaching session was that a young charmer came to me at its close and said, "You will remember to telephone me when you are eighty-nine. My fiancé has just won a cup for rifle shooting!" So if we are to be of help with the very ill, the doctors, nurses or priests must first work through their own personal view of death, especially as it eventually becomes the only adventure left.

Communication with the terminally ill pivots on this question of denial and the process may have to be explained to the relatives. Certainly bad news, be it amputation, hysterectomy or impending death, is more acceptable to the patient if it is told, even clumsily, by a loved one rather than by an outsider, however expert, but this is not always practicable. When faced with a terminally ill patient it is essential to try to assess whether they have strong denial as the majority seem to have.

Some of my colleagues claim that they would never under any circumstances indicate that an illness was terminal. The dying will accept this if they also use denial, but some would wish to share the last journey and will usually spot the deception and will no longer trust their doctor and become more miserable as a result.

Doctors at the other extreme insist on telling all their patients the truth as they see it. Again denial can come into play and the explanation is ignored. I recall asking a surgeon to see a man with an apparently operable stomach cancer. After his examination the surgeon indicated that he had told the patient the diagnosis. I went straight away to see their patient and asked what the surgeon had said, "He said that I had a duodenal ulcer that could be helped by an operation." All that is required is to be aware of and assess the denial process. We should allow the patient to tell us, rather than aggressively telling him that he is possibly dying.

I tend to sit down and ask, "What do you think about your illness?" The denier replies, "Oh I am making good progress and feel much better". The non-denier will say, "I know this must be difficult for you, doctor, but I feel that this is my last illness". It is not difficult for him as he has been allowed to decide his strategy. We then discuss the fallibility of medical diagnosis and explore the road in both directions. These patients are immensely relieved to be allowed to share their feelings and almost all will decide that the time left must be spent in repairing emotional fences with their friends and relatives rather than feeling that they must put their financial affairs in order, though that can be important too. This group are relaxed and almost happy and the helper's role almost becomes that of a midwife helping them through a second spell of labour. Some may suddenly switch back to denial for days or weeks so that considerable sensitivity and alertness is required. One lady who had been totally accepting did this type of switch and we reverted to discussing the weather. One morning I asked which was her favourite television programme and with a smile she replied, "As you know, at this stage you watch everything", and her denial did not recur.

The final journey is easier for those who have children and grandchildren as they know that part of them survives as a kind of glimpse of eternal life. The young often become extremely angry and can be almost impossible to nurse. They "rage at the dying of the light". It helps to allow them to discuss their fury at being deprived of the chance to fulfil their hopes of university, marriage, children and so on.

believe it was Thomas Mann who wisely said, "A man's dying is more the survivors' affair than his own". How the relatives cope depends on their own stability and their previous experience of bereavement. Spouses who can share the last illness without denial are indeed fortunate, but often both know the probability but try to avoid hurt by the pretence of early recovery. This seems sad if the couple have enjoyed sharing all the other joys and vicissitudes of their life together. Some people hope for a sudden death - a massive heart attack while landing a salmon. This death may be easier for the deceased than a long illness but is sometimes more difficult for the relatives. The knowledge of terminal illness will often allow an opportunity for sharing reminiscences of good times, and indeed, some of the mourning is done before the death.

Perhaps the most difficult bereavement is the loss of children. This seems especially so with deaths occurring in the late teens and twenties when so much effort has been spent in the upbringing and the results are just being fulfilled. A great deal of support and discussion is needed with the bereaved parents.

The ritual of the funeral service is important as its familiarity is reassuring and it allows a definitive end point in the process of "letting go". Problems tend to arise later if a son was abroad and unable to attend his father's funeral, or if there was no funeral as in deaths by drowning or in similar anonymous disasters.

In teaching medical students I often suggested that the reaction to bereavement can be summarised as the three Rs, perhaps especially when our parents die. The three Rs are regret, reproach and relief. Regret and sadness are normal and should be accepted and we should be able to mourn. If denial is allowed to intervene we rush around madly, interviewing undertakers, solicitors, accountants and caterers and arrange everything as a defence against mourning. Often

the mourning is only postponed. The daughter who didn
cry at her father's death will weep for a week when th
spaniel dies.

Reproach is inevitable - we feel guilty because we failed to ge
the doctor in time, or father died before the priest arrived, o
we were short tempered when he vomited - we can always
find a reason to feel guilty and this must be talked out anc
seen in proper perspective. Frequently relatives project the
guilt feeling onto the doctor or hospital and blame them, and
this we must accept or interpret depending upon the
circumstances.

Relief is the most surprising and the most difficult to
understand, so it may produce further guilt feelings. Perhaps
this feeling was given to compensate for the other two Rs. We
are relieved that the suffering is over; we are relieved that we
no longer have to trail the children to tea with granny on
Sundays; we are relieved we no longer have to explain away
our mistakes and, most important, we are relieved because at
last, "I'm a man and no longer a son".

Prognostication as to the length of life is a hazardous pastime.
I believe that we die when we have completed our life's work,
or if we are totally defeated by life. It is surprising how many
severely ill patients will survive until they see the new
grandchild, or complete some other self-selected goal. A
patient may ask, "How long have I got?" I tend to avoid the
business of prophecy if asked this question. Indeed I have
known colleagues to give an emphatic deadline for a patient
when they were in fact, unconsciously talking about their own
demise.

Controversy also rages about when to tell relatives of a
possible fatal outcome. Certainly they should, if at all
possible, be forewarned but in long illnesses the load can be
heavy and it may be wise to postpone explanations. One
woman remarked bitterly that for two years she had to buy

igarettes daily for her husband whom she knew to be slowly dying of lung cancer.

Sometimes one's instinct is to withhold information. I remember a patient whom I saw with a massive pleural effusion. I removed some of the fluids and was horrified to discover that it was full of unequivocal malignant cells confirmed by two different laboratories. I had known her husband for years and knew him to be totally dependent on his wife. I felt that it was possible he would become ill or die if I told him this news so I held my tongue. The fluid cleared completely and she is alive and well if some fifteen years older.

22. Finishing therapy

Parting is all we know of heaven
And all we need of hell.

Emily Dickinson

Parting from a patient after a psychotherapeutic relationship is often a difficult stage which requires both sensitivity and tact. I find it strange that in some areas the modern training for psychiatric registrars recommends a rigid time-limited contract, "I will see you for one year and then you must cope alone regardless". I would agree that occasionally with resistant patients it is helpful to suggest a limited contract but this is merely to stimulate them to co-operate and do some work.

As a physician I would not refuse to see a patient who developed a second bout of renal colic or pneumonia, and

since psychosomatic disorders are likely to recur in times o
crisis I think that the end of psychotherapy should leave ar
open door for the patient to return if the necessity arises.
find that this life-line is reassuring and valuable and is no
abused.

I had a letter from a former patient whose daughter was about
to have major heart surgery in London. The cardiologist had
wisely said that she, the mother, must be finding the situation
pretty stressful and she had replied, "Yes, I do, but I have a
friend in Scotland who has made me fire-proof". Another
example of the continuing life-line concerned a very
successful psychoanalyst who was admitted to hospital with
classical lobar pneumonia. She mentioned to me that every
night she was dreaming that she was driving her car and the
seat safety belts disintegrated into little fragments. I asked if
anything had happened to her own training analyst and she
replied, "Is that why I got pneumonia? He died ten days ago".

Occasionally the psychotherapy ends by the patient failing to
keep appointments or does not return after a holiday break,
leaving the therapist to wonder at the reason for this
behaviour.

Sometimes we see a paradoxical situation when the therapist
is apparently defeated and the relationship is abandoned.
One university lecturer with ulcerative colitis was so
intellectualised that she made logical and philosophical
nonsense of our discussions. I admitted defeat and we parted.
A year later she wrote to say that her symptoms cleared
completely after her final visit.

Some patients commit suicide though this is fortunately rare
in the psychosomatic field. Warning signs are usually obvious
though they may be quite subtle. One young lady sent me a
"thank you" card which bore a photograph of Marilyn
Monroe. Remembering her fate I was in time to deal with the
overdose. Another meticulous and obsessional patient sent a

cheque without having received a bill. I dashed off at once to his house but sadly he was already dead.

Normally we should stop treatment when the symptoms have abated and when the patient is enjoying a more confident and satisfying life style. Inevitably we become fond of our patients and have to guard against the temptation to keep them attending for our own dependency needs. Again the patient will provide a hint as with one lady who offered a dream that she had come to visit me in "lap-land". It is, of course, vital before parting to reassess the transference and counter transference state and to tidy up any loose ends.

So much of psychosomatic medicine is triggered by bereavement, separation or rejection that we must be very aware that finishing treatment is another bereavement, which may well cause relapse. However we usually have already discussed how the patients coped with other bereavement, and breaks in therapy for holidays are a rehearsal for the later parting. Certainly in the early stages of therapy it is vital to discuss holidays in advance of the event, since there is bound to be some dependency at this stage of treatment. The patient is liable to think that the therapist is going on holiday merely to escape from this dreadful patient. Even after full discussion the patient will say, "On the day you went on holiday I dreamt that I was stuck up a tree, and you drove off in your car, heedless of my cries for help!" So we must prepare for the parting by discussion, by spacing appointments further apart and by allowing the patient to choose the next appointment so that they can accept that they are again in control of their own life. In some of the case histories in previous chapters I have indicated the type of incidents or exchanges which suggest that the patient is ready to accept the ending of therapy.

It is useful to remember how teenagers behave when they are secure enough to leave home. Politely, or not so politely, they bring the parents down to size to indicate that they are no longer necessary for survival. A similar type of exchange is common as the end of therapy approaches and, of course, it is greatly to be welcomed as a sign of success. My day was made by one patient whose duodenal ulcer was clearly cured, and when I offered her a note of her next appointment she said, "It's all right, I always remember unimportant things!".

Often changes in the patient's fantasy life help in the process of "letting go". One patient dreamt that she came to the hospital for her appointment and I was not sitting at my desk in my white coat, but in my place there was a hospital painter eating his lunch!

A fairly unmistakable hint is not uncommon. The patient nonchalantly reports a dream in which the therapist has died. If this type of dream occurs early in the relationship, the message is quite different. It may be a panic dream that the help will not be sustained, but is usually indicating negative transference and resistance to therapy and should probably be interpreted. Towards the end of successful treatment the "death" is accepted philosophically and is often couched in terms of polite displacement. One trainee, who had learned all I could offer, had a dream that he had attended my brother's funeral and was surprised that I was not present!

At the end of treatment the therapist will also be aware of a sense of loss, but this is tempered by its similarity to that mixture of loss and triumph we experience when our children walk out of the family home, without a backward look, to fulfil their own destiny.

Appendix - clinical material

The clinical material which has provided me with experience of psychosomatic medicine was that found in inpatient and outpatient services in a large teaching hospital combined with some sessions at a peripheral district general hospital, both situated in the West of Scotland. A small element of private practice comprising two afternoons weekly provided a similar selection of patients referred for opinion on problems of internal medicine. A special interest in psychosomatic medicine made it important to remain a general physician since these psychosomatic disorders cover all areas and systems of physical disease.

From 1956 onwards I tried to keep detailed records of all psychosomatic patients seen or referred for opinion. Some of the latter category were only seen for one or occasionally two, long diagnostic interviews but did not proceed to further psychotherapy. They do, however, provide valid information on the background, personality and precipitants of the particular illness. These single interview patients were excluded from my assessment of the outcome of psychotherapy although rather unexpectedly a number subsequently reported improvement.

Up to the end of 1985 I had notes on 775 psychosomatic

patients of whom 249 (32%) had diagnostic type consultations while 526 (68%) had formal psychotherapy over periods varying widely from one month to six years. I thought that it might be interesting to examine the whole cohort of psychosomatic patients to see if they had any common features of significance. Apart from age and sex distribution, it seemed worth ascertaining if there was a family history of a related illness, or if the patients tended to have more than one psychosomatic disorder. I also tried to assess the prevalence of obsessional traits and of separation/bereavement backgrounds, since these factors seemed important from clinical experience.

(By "obsessional" I do not mean the compulsive - obsessional neurosis of psychiatric practice, but rather the virtuous obsessional, "Type A" personality who tends to be a perfectionist and who cannot leave the office until every letter is signed. Separation and bereavement include emotional separation from important friends, relatives or work situations in addition to actual death loss.)

My statistical advisor felt that some comparison with other groups of patients seen might be necessary as he somewhat mischievously suggested that my referrals were probably already selected by the family doctors. This comparison could only be done on private patients as I did not have any record of non-psychosomatic patients seen in the public service. It was agreed that a comparison between the psychosomatic patients and samples of (a) 312 patients referred for psychotherapy for non-psychosomatic conditions, and (b) 1471 patients seen as ordinary general medical referrals might be informative. The patients in the first group (a) comprised a wide variety of conditions, including hypochondriasis, alcoholism, depression, obesity and craft disorders such as writer's cramp.

These comparisons are detailed in TABLE A. It is interesting that there is a predominance of females in both psychotherapy groups but not in general referrals. I make so bold as to suggest that this is not that the female is more emotionally vulnerable but that rather that she is more courageous than the male in her efforts to achieve health and happiness. Related disorders in the close family were twice as common among psychosomatic patients and obsessional traits were also more common in this group. Bereavement was much commoner in both psychotherapy groups than in the general medical group. All these factors were statistically significant (p = 0.001).

In TABLE B I have detailed similar information to that in TABLE A. but listed under different commonly acknowledged psychosomatic disorders. These figures delineate more precisely the distribution of probably important factors in relationship to the individual disorders. Separation / bereavement is common in all disorders except ischaemic heart disease and anorexia nervosa, while the obsessional traits are very common in gastrointestinal disease, migraine and ischaemic heart disease but are less obvious in asthma, arthritis and the psychosexual disorders.

My interest in psychosomatic patients has provided a strong clinical impression that some features recur with regularity in each individual disorder although they may well vary in other cultural settings. These specific features may be useful in diagnosis and management and are discussed in the relevant chapters.

It is, of course, difficult to establish objective criteria for "cure", "improvement", or "no change in symptoms". Ideally, this should be assessed by a totally independent reviewer, but this was impracticable over such a long time-span. However, this method was employed in small groups of patients selected for other concurrent research projects (e.g. "water retention" and "peptic ulcer"). I have applied strict criteria and have downgraded the outcome unless the "cure" or "improvement" was unequivocal. By "cure" I implied that the

TABLE A

Comparison of Psychosomatic with Non-Psychosomatic Psychotherapy Patients and General Medical Referrals.

	Psychosomatic Patients	Non-Psychosomatic Patients	General Medical Referrals
	Total	Sample	Sample
	775	150/312	150/1471
Number	775	150	150
Male	295 (38%)	40 (27%)	73 (49%)
Female	480 (62%)	110 (73%)	77 (51%)
One Interview	249 (32%)	32 (21%)	137 (91%)
Family History Related Disorder	274 (35%)	26 (17%)	21 (14%)
Other Psychosomatic Disorder	255 (29%)	45 (30%)	46 (31%)
Separation / Bereavement	543 (70%)	110 (73%)	55 (37%)
"Obsessional"	462 (60%)	62 (41%)	55 (37%)
Outcome	**After**	**Psychotherapy**	**Not Applicable**
Number treated	526	118	-
Cured	96 (18%)	10 (8%)	-
Improved	389 (74%)	74 (63%)	-
Unchanged	41 (8%)	34 (29%)	-

Comparison Features of Psychosomatic Disorders

Anorexia	Arthritis	Migraine	Ischaemic heart disease	Asthma	Ulcerative colitis	Crohn's disease	Irritable Bowel Syndrome	Psychosexual	Peptic ulcer	Peptic ulcer (surgery)	
25	24	78	33	101	53	10	129	25	170	46	Number
0	7	17	26	42	18	3	34	8	88	35	Male
	29	**22**	**79**	**42**	**34**	**30**	**26**	**32**	**52**	**76**	
25	17	61	7	59	35	7	95	17	82	11	Female
00	**71**	**78**	**21**	**58**	**66**	**70**	**74**	**68**	**48**	**24**	
0	7	15	12	32	11	2	29	0	52	46	One Interview
	29	**19**	**36**	**31**	**21**	**20**	**22**		**30**	**100**	
0	4	36	14	51	17	2	38	0	87	25	Family History of Related Disorder
	17	**46**	**42**	**50**	**32**	**20**	**29**		**51**	**54**	
11	6	32	7	11	22	5	32	6	64	25	Other Psycho-somatic Disorder
44	**25**	**41**	**21**	**11**	**41.5**	**50**	**25**	**24**	**38**	**54**	
11	21	43	11	75	48	6	80	16	139	29	Separation/ Bereavement
44	**87.5**	**55**	**33**	**74**	**90**	**60**	**62**	**64**	**82**	**63**	
7	7	53	30	19	29	5	92	8	130	39	Obsessional
28	**29**	**68**	**91**	**19**	**55**	**50**	**71**	**32**	**76**	**85**	
After psychotherapy										**After Surgery**	**Outcome**
25	17	63	21	69	42	8	100	25	118	46	No.Treated
0	1	12	1	13	6	0	17	15	22	0	Cured
	6	**19**	**5**	**19**	**14**		**17**	**60**	**19**		
14	14	45	20	48	32	6	70	7	69	38	Improved
82	**82**	**71**	**95**	**69**	**76**	**75**	**70**	**28**	**58**	**83**	
11	2	6	0	8	4	2	13	3	27	8	Unchanged
44	**12**	**10**		**12**	**10**	**25**	**13**	**12**	**23**	**17**	

Percentages in Bold

patients have become totally symptom-free; those categorised as "improved" manifested only occasional symptoms after therapy. If there remained any doubt about the result, I classified the patient's condition as "unchanged".

Bibliography and references

(1)   Balint M **The Doctor, His Patient and the Ilness**
       London Pitman Medical 1964

(2)   Freud S **New Introductory Lectures on Psycho-
       Analysis** Harmondworth Penguin 1933 1973

(3)   Berne E **Transactional Analysis in Psychotherapy**
       London Evergreen Books 1961

(4)   Jung C G **Memories, Dreams and Reflections** London
       Collins & Routledge & Kegan Paul 1963

(5)   Bowlby J **Attachment and Loss** London Hogarth
       1980

(6)   Erikson E H **Childhood and Society** Harmondsworth
       Penguin 1966

(7)   Klein M **Love, Guilt and Separation** London Hogarth
       1975

(8)   Peck M Scott **The Road Less Travelled** London
       Hutchinson 1978

(9)   Rogers C **On Becoming a Person** London
       Constable 1967

(10)   Storr A **The Art of Psychotherapy** London
       Heinemann 1979

(11)   Winnicott D W **The Family and Individual
       Development** London Tavistock 1965

(12)   Lake F **Tight Corners in Pastoral Counselling**
       London Darton Longman & Todd 1974

(13)   Halliday J L **Psycho-Social Medicine.-A Study of
       the Sick Society** New York W W Norton 1948

(14)   Friedman M; Rosenman R H **Association of Specific
       Overt Behaviour Patterns with Blood and
       Cardiovascular Findings** JAMA 1959 **169** 1286-96

(15)   Paulley J W; Hughes J P **Giant Celled Arteritis or
       Arteritis of the Aged** Br. Med. J. 1960 **2** 1562-67

(16)   Bartropp R W; Luckhurst E; Lazarus H; Kilch L; Perry R
       Depressed Lymphocyte Function after Bereavement
       Lancet 1977 **1** 834-36

(17)   Hadfield J A **Dreams and Nightmares** Harmondsworth
       Penguin 1954

(18)   Graves R J **Clinical Lectures on the Practice of
       Medicine** London New Sydenham Society 1884

(19)   Quincke H **Uber Akutes Umschriebenes Hautedem**
       Monatscher. Prakt. Dermat. 1882 **1** 129-31

(20)   De Wardener H E **The Kidney** London Churchill 1967

(21)   Frank M M; Sergent J S; Kane M A; Alling D W
       Epsilon Aminocaproic Acid Therapy of Hereditary

Angio-neurotic Oedema N. Engl. J. Med. 1972 **287** 808-812

(22) Balloch Z; Whaley K **Hereditary Angio-oedema; its Pathogenesis and Management** Scott. Med. J. 1980 **3** 187-95

(23) Schottstaedt W W; Grace W J; Wolff H G **Life Situations, Behaviour, Attitudes, Emotions and Renal Excretion** J. Psychosom. Res. 1956 **1** 287-91

(24) Glen A I M; Halliburton I M; Macdonald A C **The Effect of Stress and of Mild Dehydration on Renal Solute Output in Angio-neurotic Oedema and Periodic Oedema** J. Psychosom. Res. 1969 **13** 61-66

(25) Macdonald A C **Measurements in Angio-neurotic Oedema** J. Psychosom. Res. 1964 **8** 207-211

(26) Renton C J C **Recurrent Oedema of the small Intestine** Br. J. Surg. 1965 **52** 536-539

(27) Hammer A **A Case of Thrombotic Occlusion of one of the Coronary Arteries of the Heart** Wein. med. Wohnschr 1878 **28** 102-105

(28) McNee J W **Clinical Syndrome of Coronary Arteries** Quart. J. Med. 1925 **19** 44-52

(29) Oliver M F; Boyd G S **Plasma Lipid and Serum Lipoprotein Patterns during Pregnancy and the Puerperium** Clin. Sci. 1955 **14** 15-23

(30) Arnott W **The Changing Aetiology of Heart Disease** Br. Med. J. 1954 **2** 887-891

(31) Friedmann M; Rosenman R H **Change in the Serum Cholesterol and Blood Clotting Time in men**

subjected to cyclic variations of occupational stress Circulation 1958 **17** 852-861

(32) Erskine J P O **A Case of Coronary Artery Thrombosis and Cerebral Embolism following Childbirth** J. Obst. & Gyn. 1952 **59** 844-845

(33) Sinclair-Gieben A H C; Clark C G; Dean A C B **Psychiatric Illness following surgery for Duodenal Ulcer** Scot. med. J. 1962 **7** 168-172

(34) Glen A I M **Acid Output and Personality Type in Duodenal Ulcer** J. Psychosom. Res. 1964 **8** 213-217

(35) Glen A I M **Psychotherapy and Medical Treatment for Duodenal Ulcer compared using the Augmented Histamine Test** J. Psychosom. Res. 1968 **12** 163-9

(36) Crohn B B; Ginxberg L; Oppenheimer G D **Regional Ileitis, a Pathological and Clinical Entity** JAMA 1932 **99** 1323-9

(37) Crohn B B **Granulomatous Disease of the large and small Bowel - a Historical Survey** Gastroenterology 1967 **52** 767

(38) Paulley J W **Psychotherapy in Ulcerative Colitis** Lancet 1956 **2** 215-218

(39) Paulley J W **Studies in Ulcerative Colitis** J. Psychosom. Res. 1964 **8** 89-100

(40) Paulley J W **Psychological Management of Crohn's Disease** Practitioner 1974 **213** 59-64

Index